Honda
CB750

Haynes

**Great
Bikes**

HONDA

Honda
CB750

Mick Duckworth

First published in 2003

A catalogue record for this book is available from the British Library

ISBN 1 85960 878 7

Library of Congress catalog card no. 2002110738

Published by Haynes Publishing, Sparkford,
Yeovil, Somerset, BA22 7JJ, UK

Tel: 01963 442030 Fax: 01963 440001
Int. tel: +44 1963 442030 Int. fax: +44 1963 440001
E-mail: sales@haynes-manuals.co.uk
Web site: www.haynes.co.uk

Haynes North America, Inc.,
861 Lawrence Drive, Newbury Park,
California 91320, USA

Printed and bound in England by J. H. Haynes & Co. Ltd, Sparkford

Contents

Acknowledgements

Thanks are due to the following for their help in compiling this book.

In the UK: Dave Barton and the Honda Owners Club UK, Alf Briggs, Ian Catford, Alan Cathcart, Pete Christian, *Classic Bike* and the Emap Archive, Peter Darvill, Gerald Davison, Dave Degens, David Dixon, Max Elliott, Scott Grimsdale at Honda UK, Eamon Maloney, Steve Murray, Phil Read, Tommy Robb, Derek Rickman, Chris Rushden, Bernie Saunders, Colin Seeley, the Vintage Japanese Motorcycle Club (UK), the Vintage Motor Cycle Club Library and Mick Wood.

In the USA: Patrick Bodden and Mitch Boehm of *Motor Cyclist*, Don J. Brown, David Gaylin, Bob Hansen, Mark McGrew, Jody Nicholas and Vic World.

In Australia: Jeremy Bowdler of *Two Wheels* (Australia), Ken Wootton of Australian *Motor Cycle News*, and Ken Hull.

In Germany: Frank-Albert Jllg of *Motorrad Classic*.

In Italy: Adolfo Orsi of Historica Selecta and Carlo Perelli of *Moto Ciclismo d'Epoca*.

In Sweden: Robert Laver.

Specially commissioned photography: John Colley.

Other photos and illustrations: Honda Europe, Nick Nicholls, John Noble, Jason Critchell, Alain Rouge and Mick Woollett.

Support and encouragement: Lindsay Brooke, Peter Watson and Irene De Souza.

Thanks also to Mark Hughes and the Haynes Publishing editorial team.

Note: Power output figures in this book are given in brake horsepower (bhp), but may originally have been quoted in metric PS units, which are fractionally different. For example, 60PS is equivalent to 59.16bhp.

Foreword
by Dick Mann

Winner of 24 US Grand National events 1959-72, twice AMA Grand National Champion in 1963, and 1971. Winner of the 1970 Daytona 200 on a Honda CB750 in 1970.

When I had a call from Bob Hansen asking me to ride a 750cc Honda four at Daytona in 1970, I had no idea that I was about to become part of the long and illustrious history of the Honda Motor Co. Or that the CB750 would sell in such big numbers, setting a style that everyone else wanted to follow and would eventually become a two-wheeled legend.

At the time, my job as a professional rider was to win races and I was pleased to be signed up with competitive machinery for that race in 1970. I had never competed on a Honda before, but

Dick Mann on his factory CB750 racer at Daytona International Speedway in 1970. (Steve Murray)

I knew of the company's record in grand prix racing and that it was keen for success here in the USA. Above all, Bob and I had known each other for many years in the world of racing and I could trust his depth of experience, particularly at Daytona.

The guys at Honda offered me generous terms for the one-off ride, although most of the reward depended on me winning. But that was all right with me. The race formula allowing overhead camshaft 750s like the Honda to race in the Daytona 200 was new that year, and I had never ridden a four-cylinder motorcycle before. So I was glad to find that it rode well.

Daytona is a rough ride and very brutal on engines because you hold maximum speed for such long periods. My job was to get that bike to the finish first and I was pleased with the result – longer races were always my forte. It put a couple of years on my career, too, because I'd proved that I wasn't over the hill, as some people seemed to think.

Mick Duckworth has not been around the motorcycle scene as long as I have, but I know him and his work, and feel sure you will enjoy reading this book about the fascinating history of the Honda CB750 Four. It can truly be called a Great Bike.

Dick Mann

Dick Mann
Gardnerville, Nevada

Introduction

Honda's CB750 Four ranks among that elite of machines that can claim to be the most important in the whole of motorcycling history.

Bursting on to the scene in 1969, Honda's first four-cylinder roadster revolutionised the large-capacity market. Its advanced specification, scintillating performance and eye-catching style made everything else in volume production look archaic is comparison.

Able to cruise effortlessly on the autobahn, interstate or motorway, the potent CB750 had scorching top-end acceleration by 1960s' standards, accompanied by an exhilarating exhaust note previously heard only at grand prix races. Compared with traditional twin-cylinder high-performance bikes of its day, the Four was smooth, highly reliable and easy to live with.

The CB750 was also historically significant because it marked the Japanese industry's arrival in the large-capacity motorcycle field. And it proved that Honda could put what was then seen as an exotic design in showrooms at an affordable price.

A huge seller, the CB750 enjoyed an unusually long production life. It was enormously influential, setting a trend so enthusiastically followed by other makers that customers soon took the blend of speed, convenience and reliability for granted. Eventually, there were so many capable, four-cylinder imitators at large that they earned the 'Universal Japanese Motorcycle' label.

This prompted Honda to diversify, most notably with its admired 750cc V-four engines. Yet to this day, the company's most outstanding super sport designs such as the FireBlade and CBR600F follow the transverse four layout pioneered by the CB750.

Considering it was more a 'grand tourer', than a super sport, the CB750 enjoyed a surprising degree of racing success, especially when its stock frame was replaced by a chassis designed to provide improved handling to suit circuit use.

The story of the great Honda CB750 is a fascinating one, which starts right here . . .

The giant step

Today, we take the reliable high-performance motorcycle for granted. Dealer's showrooms are packed with superb machinery that can be ridden for mile after mile at high speed with a minimum of attention. Free-revving, smooth-running, multi-cylinder engines are commonplace and we expect to ride over long distances without discomfort or fatigue.

The sophisticated modern product is the result of a long evolutionary process that can be traced back to experiments with crude powered two-wheelers built in the late 19th century. Over the succeeding years of continual development there were particular machines which made leaps rather than mere steps in technical and marketing progress. And among that small number, one motorcycle stands out as the biggest leap of all: the Honda CB750.

Unveiled as the CB750 Dream Four at the 1968 Tokyo Motor Show, Honda's momentous model offered a dazzling array of features previously unheard of on a mass-produced motorcycle. It was a remarkable package of performance, style, quality and affordability.

From that moment, motorcycles would have to meet heightened levels of customer expectations. Riders would never again need to accept that harsh engine vibration, unscheduled stoppages and persistent oil leaks were the inevitable corollary of owning a machine capable of 120mph (193km/h).

A well-kept secret up until shortly before its sensational launch, the four-cylinder Honda instantly became the favourite talking point of motorcyclists the world over. It also sent shock waves through the industry, especially the older factories outside Japan which had previously had the over-500cc market to themselves.

Even Honda's arrival on the 'big bike' scene in 1966 with its largest capacity machine to date, the CB450 twin, failed to shake their complacency. While Japan had become the world's largest motorcycle producer, Western manufacturers perceived its factories as being firmly focused on a market for small bikes.

They were well aware that Honda, the biggest maker on the planet since 1967, made and sold reliable utility runabouts by the tens of thousands. They grudgingly admired the zippy two-stroke gems turned out by Bridgestone, Kawasaki, Suzuki and Yamaha. But many in the old industry remained convinced that the high-value, large displacement motorcycle for the mature, committed rider was in a province of its own.

A typical choice of over-500cc machine for a keen motorcyclist in the mid-1960s would have been a parallel twin from BSA, Norton or Triumph with overhead valves operated by pushrods. The most popular of these was Triumph's 650cc T120 Bonneville, a strong seller both at home and on the lucrative North American market. With lively, 110mph-plus (177+km/h) performance, the Triumph was also admired for its agile handling and lean symmetrical looks. But, like the other British twins it had an drawback in the form of vibration, the result of an inherently unbalanced engine layout which became more obtrusive as engine size increased.

The tremors made life uncomfortable for the long-distance rider and had infuriating side-

Show stealer: the CB750 Four and an engine during its sensational 1968 Tokyo Show debut. (Honda)

Honda's first HQ in Hamamatsu. (Honda)

effects, such as wrecking delicate – and expensive – parts of the charging system, blowing light bulbs, loosening fasteners and occasionally even fracturing cycle parts such as mudguard stays.

Other problems arose thanks to the weakness of items such as the electrical switchgear and carburettors sourced from outside suppliers at rock-bottom prices. Build quality was often poor and any owner regularly covering high mileages at over 60mph (97km/h) was likely to face a continual repair programme and the constant challenge of stemming oil leaks.

The more far-sighted designers within the British industry wanted to improve the product, but their employers were unable to contemplate anything really innovative because chronic lack of

investment had left them stuck with antiquated plant and manufacturing methods.

As early as 1960, the BSA-Triumph group boss Edward Turner had visited the well-equipped Japanese factories, including a Honda plant, so the UK industry had some idea of what could be in store. Turner retired in 1964 and the ostrich-like line increasingly adopted by British industry spokesmen was that they were happy to see the Japanese turning out ever-greater numbers of lightweights, since those who rode them would naturally graduate to large-capacity machines produced by British companies.

Harley-Davidson, America's last surviving volume producer, had taken the precaution of buying into the Italian Aermacchi company to

A major milestone in 20th century motorcycling, the Honda
Dream Four as it was unveiled in 1968. (Honda)

maintain a presence in the lightweight market. Its over-500 range of heavyweight V-twins had changed little in decades, although electric starting had been introduced on the lumbering 95mph (153km/h) 1,200cc Electra Glide. The leaner, 883cc XLCH Sportster was ambitiously claimed to exceed 120mph, but not in comfort.

Another mid-1960s option was BMW. The German factory, then recovering from near-bankruptcy, had stuck firmly with a horizontally opposed 'boxer' twin-cylinder engine format since the 1920s. This had the virtue of being well balanced and therefore smooth-running. But, while BMW's 600cc ohv sports tourer with shaft drive offered quality and refinement it had a staid image, was highly priced in most markets and made in comparatively small numbers.

Italy had traditionally concentrated on light-weights, with the odd 500cc range-topper. But Moto Guzzi, then the nation's biggest factory, launched an innovative 704cc V7 V-twin tourer in 1966. Its sturdy engine had been developed with government funding provided for an all-terrain military vehicle.

Within months of the CB450's appearance, rumours permeated the industry to the effect that Honda was working on an even larger capacity motorcycle, generally assumed to be a parallel twin on similar lines.

Mass produced fours were widely regarded as the stuff of fantasy. British designers knew that a four-cylinder engine with its inherent balance would give a super smooth ride but were con-vinced such a unit was too bulky for a sports machine. Their management took the view that the consumer did not need multi-cylinder engines, which along with overhead camshafts were seen as unnecessary extravagance, best left to foreign racing teams.

Four-cylinder machines had competed in grand prix road racing since pre-war times, but

they were created in tiny numbers by small teams of factory technicians. Stirring spectators with their bellowing unsilenced exhausts, they were usually only seen close-up by holders of pit passes at international races, which served to boost their mystique. Yet Gilera and Moto Guzzi, two of the leading Italian factories to field multi-cylinder racers in the 1950s, had not attempted to market road versions. Indeed, they withdrew from racing to concentrate on selling comparatively mundane machines to the public.

Harley-Davidson built a 1,000cc concept bike with a mocked-up double overhead camshaft in-line four-cylinder engine in 1966, but the project was dumped because it was thought to lack commercial potential.

Ducati, the Italian government-owned lightweight four-stroke specialist had unveiled a futuristic 1,260cc V-four in 1964, but it failed to reach production. BMW saw no reason to abandon its beloved boxer twin.

However, there were two four-cylinder 100mph motorcycles on the market when the Honda CB750 was launched. The Italian MV Agusta company, famous for its grand prix racing successes with machines built regardless of cost and bearing no relation to showroom models, released a roadgoing double overhead camshaft in-line four in 1966. Clearly intended as a 'Gran Tourismo' machine, the 600cc twin-carburettor MV had shaft final drive and rather ungainly styling with a rectangular Fiat car headlamp.

Admired by many for its modernity and sophistication, the 250cc CB72 twin of 1960 was mocked by detractors for being a 'cissy' bike. (Honda)

With nothing like the shattering performance of MV's racers, the 600 was expensive and availability was restricted, fewer than 200 examples being sold during the five years it was listed. Years earlier, MV had dropped a bombshell by displaying a 500cc four-cylinder shaft-drive tourer at the 1950 Milan Show, but that never reached production.

The rarely seen Münch Mammoth 4 was created by the entrepreneurial German Friedl Münch and unveiled in 1967. Appropriately named and extremely weighty, the Mammoth was powered by an air-cooled NSU 1,085cc in-line four-cylinder car engine installed across the frame.

Its claimed performance of 137mph (220km/h) outstripped any existing production motorcycle by a large margin, and the price was astronomical, too: being no less than three times that of a 650cc Triumph.

Honda's main men

Soichiro Honda

The 750cc Four project typified Soichiro Honda's bold attitude to technical innovation, while being made possible by Takeo Fujisawa's prudent planning and financial management.

'Pop' Honda's grounding in automotive technology stretched back to long before his founding of the Honda Motor Company. Born in 1906, he was fascinated by machinery from an early age, hanging out in his father's smithy and bicycle repair workshop in a village near Hamamatsu.

In his teens, he took an apprenticeship at a garage in Tokyo. One of its few staff to survive the devastating earthquake of 1923, Soichiro helped rebuild the business before setting up on his own account in 1928. Encouraged by racing driver Shinichi Sakibahara, he hand-built his own car around an American Curtiss V8 aero engine. This was the first in a series of racing cars he created and Honda proved himself no mean driver, too. He was lucky to escape from a high-speed crash when competing at Tama River, near Tokyo in 1936. He rolled his supercharged Ford-powered car several times, moments after setting a new lap record.

Following this incident, Soichiro gave up racing and applied his prodigious energy to setting up a factory to make piston rings, much needed during Japan's massive armaments build-up.

After a faltering start, his products attained sufficient quality to gain contracts with aircraft and truck companies. During the Second World War, the plant was bombed in the war and further damaged by another earthquake in 1945.

When Japan surrendered, Honda took a realistic view of the situation. He sold out to Toyota and took a long sabbatical, to relax and take stock of his future in a war-ravaged country. Refreshed by the break, he set up the tiny enterprise in Hamamatsu that would become the Honda Motor Company.

Honda rated practical experience above paper qualifications and staff suggestion schemes were introduced in the factories as early as 1953. But his brusque and sometimes irascible manner did not always go down well with employees.

It is possible that his 1954 decision to launch into international racing was partly prompted by growing unrest among employees, at a time when staffing levels were escalating dramatically. Sporting projects could rally a youthful and restless workforce behind the Honda banner.

There are stories of 'Pop' Honda throwing tools around when angry and even assaulting members of his staff. But he also knew how to escape and unwind, counting art, hang-gliding and skiing among his various hobbies.

After retiring from the company presidency on Honda's 25th anniversary in 1973, Soichiro distanced himself from the running of the company, believing his successors should have free rein. He had actively avoided coaching his son or any other family members to take his place. Soichiro Honda died in 1991, aged 84.

Soichiro Honda (left) with Takeo Fujisawa (Honda).

Takeo Fujisawa

Astute and business-like yet ready to take measured risks, Takeo Fujisawa provided a perfect foil to the flamboyant creativity of Mr Honda, and must take much of the credit for nursing the company through critical years in the 1950s. It was also he who implemented a dynamic response to Honda's falling US sales in the period immediately prior to the launch of the CB750.

Four years Soichiro Honda's junior, Fujisawa joined the fledgling Honda Motor Company as managing director in 1948 and kept a firm hand on the tiller to steer it safely through years of dramatic expansion.

Like Honda, Fujisawa gained expertise through hard experience and not at academic institutions. His family was left destitute by the 1923 earthquake and after a deprived childhood, he served in the army. He then joined a Tokyo-based steel supply company where he honed his sales expertise and took over its running prior to the outbreak of war.

It was Fujisawa who, in the early days, masterminded the massive expansion of Honda's dealer network and urged constant refinement of the product. To head off the threat of souring industrial relations in the mid-1950s, he addressed the entire workforce at a mass meeting in 1954 and convinced them of the company's case.

In 1964, he became the company's vice president and set up Honda's unusual joint boardroom system, whereby up to 30 senior executives shared a single office space. Like Honda, Fujisawa did not subscribe to the strict hierarchies traditionally favoured in Japan, understanding that too much 'top-down' management could suppress creativity and innovation.

Although Honda was technically Fujisawa's senior, the two men acted more as equals and had a strong, although by no means always harmonious, personal relationship. The two men even retired on the same date in 1973.

Although Honda's public image was of a technically bold outfit capable of building the most intricate and powerful four-stroke racers, it was not expected to dabble in producing exclusive novelties for a handful of rather wealthy enthusiasts.

But build a four it did, and to understand how Honda dared to go into production with the kind of dream machine that older companies shied away from, we should look at the previous history of the company.

Company founder Soichiro Honda was a man given to original thinking and with more than a dash of the maverick in his outlook. He did not fit with a stereotypical view of the Japanese as ultra-conformist and deferential to authority. Although well-grounded in the harsh realities of manufacturing Honda always admired lateral thinking and never lost faith in the abstract concepts of motivation and aspiration. Tellingly, a whole progression of Honda motorcycles from the Fifties to the Seventies used the Dream model name applied to the CB750. It's still a key word in Honda publicity today, the company's current global slogan being The Power of Dreams.

It is now a matter of legend that Mr Honda started out in the two-wheeler business in the 1940s by fitting surplus ex-military generator engines to bicycles and subsequently developing his own rather basic single-cylinder two-stroke engine.

The Honda Model A, with its rudimentary motor slung under the crossbar and driving the rear wheel by belt, proved popular in a country devastated by war and desperately short of basic transport. In the latter part of 1948, Soichiro Honda had gathered together sufficient capital to found the Honda Motor Company in Hamamatsu. By taking on Takeo Fujisawa as his sales and finance chief, he embarked on a partnership that would prove to be as dynamic and successful as any in automotive history.

Honda refined its 'clip-on' bicycle engines and they became hot sellers, bringing in useful revenue. The first real Honda motorcycle was the 100cc Model D Dream two-stroke of 1950, followed two years later by the 150cc Model E. This had an overhead valve engine and marked the start of a long period in which Honda only made two-wheelers with four-stroke power units.

Giant four: the German Münch 4 in its 1971 form. (*Motorrad Classic*)

The Model J of 1953 had tidier looks and showed significant technical progress. The first Honda to bear the long-running model name 'Bendy', meaning convenient and later modified to Benly for obvious reasons, it was similar in general profile to the German NSU company's sturdy single-cylinder models. The gearbox was built in unit with the engine and the spine-type frame fabricated from steel pressings. Its capacity was 90cc, then a popular category in Japan.

Honda sales slumped due to recession in Japan in the wake of the Korean War, while labour disputes were spreading throughout the country. But a remarkable recovery effort by both management and workforce saw Honda bounce back and forge ahead to become the nation's

biggest motorcycle manufacturer in 1955. The next target would be the company's expansion into world markets.

A department purely concerned with research and development was opened in 1957 and two very significant models appeared in the following year. One was the 250cc C71 which was similar to the 1957 C70, Honda's first overhead camshaft parallel twin, but featured electric starting. In doing away with the usual kick-starting method this refinement made the Honda more attractive to the public as a whole, even though it might have been scorned by hardened macho bikers.

Even more important was the C100 Super Cub, a cross between a motorcycle and a scooter designed to be economical, convenient and clean. It had a small, 50cc four-stroke engine with

a near-horizontal cylinder, looking rather like a miniature of the Italian Aermacchi unit. With comprehensive mudguarding, leg shields and full enclosure of the power unit and drive chain, the C100's 'step-thru' layout made it supremely easy to use by anyone, male or female and regardless of dress. But unlike a scooter, it had large diameter wheels that rode well over bad surfaces.

While not really revolutionary, the user-friendly and dependable Super Cub turned out to be a stroke of genius. Cleverly targeted at a gap in the market, it sold and sold and sold. The C100 and its various 50, 70 and 90cc derivatives went on to become the most prolific and enduring two-wheeler of all time – more than five million had been sold when CB750 development started, and the total figure has now exceeded 30 million.

Ideal for markets where rugged utilitarian two-wheelers were in demand for basic transport, the 'Honda Fifty' also assumed the role of a fun machine in more affluent environments. Its

commercial success earned Honda revenue with which to develop more specialised and sport-orientated products such as the CB750.

The original CB range of sporty motorcycles with twin-cylinder, twin-carburettor single overhead camshaft engines was initiated in 1959 to admirers in the world's main motorcycle markets. Not everyone warmed to their unfamiliar angular styling, but the CB twins' smooth, quiet operation, cleanliness and ease of maintenance set high standards that impressed owners and gave rival makers a warning.

From 1963, the 305cc CB77 had been added to the range and established itself as the definitive entry-level machine for young riders in the USA, where it sold under the Super Hawk model name. By 1964, Honda had a 62 per cent share of the American motorcycle market. Also, in defiance of the Japanese government's industrial strategy the company had waded into the car and light truck market and with typical boldness had entered the Formula One car racing arena.

The steady rise up the motorcycle cubic capacity ladder saw the CB450, considered Honda's first real 'big bike', launched in 1965. But ever since the 1950s, US dealers had urged British factories to build bikes with engines of 750cc, a size familiar to experienced Stateside riders because native makers Harley-Davidson and Indian had traditionally listed 45cu in (750cc) models.

CB450: high-technology twin

Targeted mainly against the popular British 650 twins, Honda's CB450 aimed to equal them on performance through superior technology and higher rpm rather than on cubic capacity.

Like many of the earlier CB's engines the 444cc unit was a parallel twin with crankshaft throws spaced at 180 intervals but the twin overhead camshafts, usually associated with ultimate-performance racing engines, were new. Also novel was the use of torsion bars to close the valves in place of coil springs. Unlike earlier CB twins and most of Honda's GP racing engines, it featured vertical cylinders.

Weighty for the 500cc class at 187kg (412lb) dry, the 450 had peaky rather than fluid power delivery and did not deliver the sensational top-end performance that was promised.

In the UK, an advertising agency coined the name 'Black Bomber' for the 450. It also stoked up controversy with an aggressive advertising campaign in the motorcycling press, comparing the modern CB450 with antiquated British designs.

Despite this, the Black Bomber sales were so disappointing in the UK that one leading Honda dealer, Ken Ives of Leicester, refinished some CB450s in bright red to help move them out of the showroom.

In the USA the twin's styling, especially the shape of what the factory called the 'tuna tank' deterred sales, as did a lack of Triumph-like tractability. But Honda responded to criticism and the 450 did much better after it acquired a restyled fuel tank and a five-speed gearbox in 1968.

It was joined by a CL450 street scrambler version at the same time and both models lived on in the US and other markets such as Germany, until 1972.

Honda's first venture into over-350cc territory, the CB450 twin. Its styling and buzzy engine put off traditional 'big bike' buyers. (Honda)

As a nation, the Japanese tend to be of small stature, but Soichiro Honda apparently became convinced that a 'jumbo' motorcycle could be viable, during a visit to the States. He noticed that American riders of very large build could dwarf even machines of 650cc. On his return to Japan, he initiated a development programme for what became known at Honda as the 'King of Motorcycles'.

Yoshirou Harada, who had been responsible for design and development of the CB72 and CB450 twins was in charge of the big bike project. He recalls seven guidelines given to his team of 20 technicians at the outset:

1. A highway cruising speed of between 85 and 100mph. A broad power band with minimum vibration and engine noise. A high degree of safety.
2. Excellent stability, even when travelling at over 100mph.
3. Strong and reliable braking, effective at high speed and with full loading.
4. Ergonomic riding position and controls, for a relaxed and comfortable ride.
5. Lighting and instrumentation which is patently sophisticated and reliable. Overall looks that will get the machine noticed by other road users.
6. Utter reliability from every component, while inspection and maintenance must be easy.
7. Full use of new materials, technologies and the latest surface treatments to ensure unique design and promote ease of production.

Harada's team was able to refer to a mass of documentation arising out of the grand prix racing campaign. Honda's research and development department had the most

The American Dream

When Honda set out to become a worldwide marque in the 1950s, the company's market researchers suggested it would be best to concentrate on Europe and Southeast Asia rather than North America. The reasoning behind this was based on US two-wheeler sales running at a disappointing 50,000 a year (compared with Honda's own 1959 output of 500,000 units) in a market of 150,000,000 people.

Sales were to some extent hindered by the poor public image of motorcycles in the USA, where they were closely associated with gang culture and anti-social behaviour. The only major American manufacturer, Harley-Davidson, had some interest in keeping the market small to help maintain control of it through national trade and sport associations.

But Takeo Fujisawa was insistent that Honda should target America, on the basis that any company seeking worldwide credibility had to be seen to thrive in the biggest and most developed consumer market of all. A product that made discerning US customers happy could succeed anywhere else in the world. Since the bulk of US two-wheeler sales at that time were in the larger capacity bracket, there seemed to be little competition for Honda's smaller machines.

American Honda was set up in small premises on Pico Boulevard, Los Angeles in June 1959. Southern California was a sensible choice of location, since a growing and affluent population combined with a largely dry climate to make it a centre of motorcycling activity. Also, it was where most ships carrying goods from Japan were unloaded. Kihachiro Kawashima, who had joined Honda in 1951, ran the operation.

Initially it was a tough market to crack and only 2,500 machines were sold in 1960.

One difficulty lay in getting the motorcycle trade to take Honda's projected sales seriously and it was found that many dealers were catering to an exclusive sub-culture of 'real men' who took pride in mastering unwieldy and quirky machines that required endless fettling to deliver reliable high performance. Shop staff sporting black fingernails and oily overalls were not likely to sell step-throughs to smartly dressed men and women.

The answer was to by-pass biker culture, setting up the first dealerships in sports shops and hardware stores rather than established bike shops, and in 1962, Honda made the breakthrough that paved the way for real success. Working with the LA advertising agency Gray Inc, the company launched a nation-wide campaign to sell the C100 step-thru, based on the now-legendary slogan: 'You Meet the Nicest People on a Honda'. Placed in a variety of general interest magazines such as *Life*, Honda's lively advertisements succeeded in creating a positive, friendly and upbeat image.

Sales of the expanding range built up as Honda established itself as a familiar and trusted brand. In 1964, the company spent $350,000 – half its annual advertising budget – on two 90-second TV commercials. Screened during the annual Academy Awards presentation, they paid off in sales and by the end of that year American Honda had wrested more than 60 per cent of the nation-wide two-wheeler market and was selling well over 100,000 units per year.

Elvis Presley rode a Honda Super Hawk in his 1964 movie *Roustabout* and in the same year The Hondells had a US Top Five hit singing *Little Honda*, a song written by Brian Wilson of the Beach Boys.

Marketing reliable and easy-to-use trail bikes popularised Honda among fishermen, hunters and farmers as well as weekend sport riders. However, road riders for whom motorcycling was a major long-term interest felt the need to graduate from the 250s and 350-class machines on which they learned their road skills.

The CB450 went some way to satisfy this need but buyers were put off by unfamiliar styling and a buzzy character that distanced it from mainstream big bikes like the nimble, torquey and elegant 650cc Triumph Bonneville.

Honda weathered a sales recession in 1966 and '67, but recovered in 1968 partly thanks to

(Photograph courtesy of Honda)

strong sales of the Z50 Mini Trail aimed at young riders and the launch of the CB350 twin, a hot seller despite being branded as dull and unexceptional by sporting riders.

BSA and Triumph, and to a lesser extent Norton, were supplying the US market with nimble high-performance 650cc twins, and from late in 1968, some 750cc triples. That year, BSA and Triumph together sold 40,944 units of all types, against Honda's 181,105 and Harley-Davidson's 26,834.

Italian factories were limbering up to go after American sales, led by the American Eagle-badged Laverda twin, available through a network of more than 750 dealers.

Financially troubled Harley-Davidson was rescued by the American Machine & Foundry Company (AMF) late in 1968 but production of its big V-twins was not interrupted.

As the leading marque in the arena by a considerable margin, Honda could scarcely afford not to offer a large-capacity model. Along with other Japanese makes it had successfully sold smaller machines to the 18-26 age group and saw the widespread trade-up to large capacity motorcycles developing. Why sit back and let Triumph, Harley-Davidson and the rest sell all the big bikes?

sophisticated equipment available, including electronic sensors and meters to analyse engine functions during bench tests. A high-speed film camera recorded combustion events through quartz windows in cylinder heads and, significantly, all data could be processed through computers.

Masaru Shirakura, the engineer in charge of creating the power unit recalled that at the outset, no specific engine displacement was stipulated.

'We were simply told: "the bigger, the better." We began by looking at how to reduce vibration in a large engine, so the machine could be ridden for very long periods without being uncomfortable or tiring. For a parallel twin, the upper size limit level before vibration became a real problem seemed to be 500cc, so we discussed the use of vee or horizontally opposed cylinder layouts and what sort of torque fluctuation effects they might have on machine stability.'

The decision to go ahead with an in-line four-cylinder design came in February 1968. Bob Hansen, who had joined American Honda in 1960 becoming a key figure at the head office in California, is sure it was he who convinced Soichiro Honda himself to go for a four. He recalled: 'A small group of us went to Japan to visit the factory early in 1968. We were due to meet Mr Honda but were told he would be late, because he was having his English lesson. So in the meantime they took us on a tour of the R&D department, but our guide said he couldn't let us see the test area, because they didn't want anyone to see the engine they were developing for a new large capacity motorcycle. The word was that a new 750cc twin was under way and I had the idea its motor might be based on the existing N360 car engine.

'Then we had our meeting with Mr Honda and I was talking to him through an interpreter, because that was best way to study his facial reactions. He said they were going to build what

he called the King of Motorcycles. I have always believed in speaking my mind, and I said to him: "That's good – I hope it's not a twin". He looked at me and said: "Why do you say that?"

'I replied that if Honda was to build the King of Motorcycles it had to be a four, not just another twin. A four-cylinder road bike didn't seem such a big deal to me at the time, because they had been around years before and Honda had raced plenty of fours.'

Hansen later received a letter from Harada which acknowledged that it was he who persuaded Honda to build a four.

Shirakura recalled how his team set out to minimise the drawbacks of a big engine, such as bulky appearance, excessive weight and extreme complexity: 'Various comparative studies were done with layout drawings and wooden models. The frontal area of the machine, its weight and tyre sizes were estimated in calculating the engine power curve needed to maintain it at a cruising speed of around 100mph.

'In the earliest stages of development, the machine's dimensions – especially its width – would have made it impossible to ride. By placing the camshaft and primary drives in the centre and using a multi-shaft gearbox the engine width at leg height was kept down to near that of a twin-cylinder engine. To reduce the height, we tilted the cylinders forward by 15°.

'A single forged crankshaft supported by five plain bearings was chosen rather than a complex built-up assembly. A dry sump lubrication system took away the need for a deep sump in the bottom of the engine, and helped to reduce its height.

'Once we had decided on the basic layout we hit upon the idea of placing the starter at the rear of the crankshaft, and the oil filter in front. Perhaps we should have applied for a patent on this arrangement, as it later became the norm on Japanese four-cylinder motorcycle engines.'

Track lessons

A successful grand prix racing campaign from 1961 to 1967 had provided a wealth of experience and data for Honda to draw on in developing a four-cylinder roadster engine. The company's first track venture was a disappointing outing in Brazil during 1954, but later that year Soichiro Honda attended the Isle of Man TT races to assess the level of technology involved.

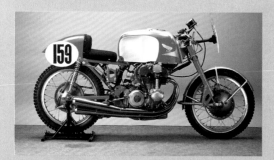

Honda's very first four, the 250cc RC160, which won a national Japanese race on the roughly surfaced Asama circuit in 1959. (Honda)

He was deeply impressed, particularly by multi-cylinder Italian machinery and the German NSUs then dominant in the 125 and 250cc classes. He vowed to return to the Island with a Honda team.

The TT debut came five years later when twin-cylinder Hondas put on a display of consistency, if not speed, to finish in sixth, seventh, eighth and tenth places in the 1959 125cc race.

In August of that year, Honda wheeled out its first four-cylinder racer with a 250cc in-line double overhead camshaft engine. The RC160 won at Japan's rough-surfaced Asama track and was the precursor of an amazing series of high-revving, multi-cylinder machines to be fielded by Honda in succeeding years.

The company won its first world championships in 1961 with a 125cc twin and a 250cc four and then, as Honda came under increasing pressure from Suzuki and Yamaha's rapidly developing two-strokes, it developed 50cc twins, a five-cylinder 125 and the revolutionary six-cylinder 250 first aired in 1965. Committed to four-stroke technology, Honda sought maximum output by using multiple cylinders of small individual capacity each with four valves rather than the normal two, disposed around a central spark plug. Using a short crankshaft stroke gave a relatively large bore size, enabling valve area to be maximised, while reciprocating weight in the twin camshaft valve gear was kept very low in the interest of maintaining high rpm.

The 1966 50cc RC116 twin gave its maximum power at a giddy 21,500rpm, unprecedented for a four-stroke motorcycle engine. No wonder such

intricate designs were often described as 'wrist-watch engineering'.

Honda chassis design was unremarkable, with tubular frames, telescopic forks and drum brakes, but care was taken to minimise frontal area for aerodynamic efficiency.

When Honda arrived on the GP scene, the larger 350 and 500cc capacity classes were ruled by MV Agusta. The proud Italian factory was soon toppled in the 350cc category, where Honda took every title from 1962 to 1967, but the 500cc Blue Riband class proved harder to crack.

Honda's first 500cc GP contender was an 85bhp four, notoriously too powerful for its chassis and consequently an atrocious handler. Nevertheless, in 1966, the RC181's first GP year, it took the manufacturer's championship in its class, giving Honda a unique grand slam of five such titles in that season.

When Honda decided to withdraw from the world championships after 1967 it had notched up more than 130 grand prix victories. The success boosted the company's public image as a leader in motorcycle technology and the fabulous racers had become legendary. The promise of owning a four-cylinder road machine from the same stable as the famous howling GP multis was one of the CB750's great attractions.

Typically, Honda GP engines of the 1960s had inclined cylinders and gear-driven double overhead camshafts, like this 1961 250cc four. (Honda)

Although Honda obviously drew on its racing experience with four-cylinder engines, the double overhead camshaft layout they had used in track engines to obtain high rpm and maximum output per cc of displacement was not employed on the 750cc engine. According to Harada, this was because his horsepower target was to better that claimed for the most potent Harley-Davidson twins, which was approximately 60bhp. Honda knew this could be achieved with a less-costly and more-easily serviced layout. A single overhead camshaft, driven by chain from the centre of the crankshaft, as it was on the N360 car engine, was preferred. Harada has also recalled that he had anticipated a dohc version being introduced two or three years after the first model's launch.

Clothing the King was the job of designer Hitoshi Ikeda, whose philosophy was to make the styling of a vehicle complement its functions.

'A good design makes the onlooker feel the performance and efficiency of the bike without even riding it. If a motorcycle's engine is on view, it needs to be imposing. One way of helping achieve this is to design a fuel tank that is slim and does not overshadow the engine, making it more noticeable as a result.

'In designing the CB750 Four, I looked mainly to the American market, where at that time British products were the most popular sports bikes. The original CB450, which had a German-style fuel tank reflecting the tastes of Soichiro Honda, had not been well received in America. So I proceeded with a more evolutionary design, focusing on the image of an ideal motorcycle as an American rider might envisage it.

'It was also necessary that the Four was to give the immediate impression of being a direct linear descendent of our grand prix racers. Basing the whole around the four-cylinder engine with four separate megaphone-shaped exhaust pipes, I set out to create a wild, dynamic image in keeping with the high-handlebar style favoured by Americans.

'We looked into using a rolled-tube silencer construction, but eventually adopted a two-piece, pressed-sheet structure which could be formed more easily. This was important because it was necessary to incorporate complex curves into the tubing to keep the system as compact as possible.'

Hansen recalls a discussion with Soichiro Honda with regard to the Four's exhaust system: 'I told him it might be quieter and maybe more efficient as a four-into-one system, but for maximum sales appeal it needed to have four mufflers (silencers).'

At the time that the CB750 was under development, Soichiro Honda and Takeo Fujisawa were deeply pre-occupied with the Honda 1300 car project, which was problematic enough to strain the two men's working relationship and ultimately make a loss in the showroom. But Mr Honda showed up occasionally to see how work was progressing on his King of Motorcycles.

Checking over an early prototype engine, his attention was drawn to the oil filter, which at that point was housed in the clutch casing. He asked one of the young engineers working on the project to show him how easily its element could be changed. When it was withdrawn he saw that it was contaminated with grease and was so angry that he struck the poor technician on the head.

Mr Honda also apparently jibed at his test riders, who were of small build, as the majority of Japanese men were in the Sixties, saying that they would be like insects sitting on such a big machine and that perhaps they should invite American riders to test it.

Like many leading motorcycle factories, Honda tended to focus on engine technology more than chassis design. But the 750 Four power unit needed a sound set of cycle parts to fulfil its brief as an easy-to-ride, stable motorcycle with ample braking power.

For the first time on a road model, Honda used a double cradle frame. Moving away from the 250 and 305 CB twins' type, with the engine carried beneath a pressed-steel spinal member, the CB450 had a tubular cradle frame with a single front downtube. The 750's tubular structure went a stage further with twin lower tubes supporting the relatively wide engine cases. A conventional design for the period, it followed a layout similar to that employed by leading European makers on larger capacity machines.

Right up until its public unveiling at the 1968 Tokyo Motor Show, the CB750 was being tested with drum brakes on the front and rear wheels. But, at a late stage, the decision was taken to equip the machine with a disc front brake.

By the mid-1960s, brakes that operated by using a hydraulic system to press friction pads against a metal disc fixed to the wheel hub were being widely adopted in the four-wheeled world, but still rare on motorcycles. Some Italian road race teams were experimenting with disc brakes made by the Campagnolo company, which were also fitted to MV Agusta's 600 roadster four. However, they were cable-operated and the pioneer of hydraulic units on two-wheelers was American racer Al Gunter. A brilliant rider and engineer, he fitted discs to his single-cylinder BSAs using Hurst Airheart hydraulic components supplied to constructors of midget cars raced on US oval tracks.

Bob Hansen recalled that when Mr Harada was in America during testing of the CB72, he had asked to see Gunter's brake which had cable-operated frame-mounted master cylinders.

Honda had approached Hurst Airheart with a view to commissioning production of components, but in the event decided to devise its own disc brake in collaboration with Japanese hydraulics specialist Tokico. Its operation was similar to that of the Girling pin-slider type brake first seen on cars in 1966.

To plan and develop such a radical new motorcycle in a matter of months was pretty fast work, which reflects the pitch of creativity and efficiency that Honda had achieved in the company's relatively short life. The company also had experience of meeting tight schedules in the chase to stay competitive during a tough grand prix racing campaign. The celebrated six-cylinder 250cc GP racer had been taken from drawing board to test track in less than three months.

By comparison, the development schedule of Britain's 750cc triples, the Honda's principal rivals in the American market, seems woefully slow. A three-cylinder engine was first drawn up at Triumph in 1963, but it was not until October 1968 before the BSA Rocket 3 and Triumph T150T Trident were unveiled to the public.

Triumph's original triple engine was not a wholly new design like Honda's 750 but a test rig based closely on existing engines, virtually a 500cc twin with an extra cylinder added. According to *Whatever Happened to the British Motorcycle Industry?*, by former BSA and Triumph executive Bert Hopwood, the experimental 750cc triple was only made a production priority after the BSA-Triumph board was warned that Honda was rumoured to be planning a 750cc motorcycle.

Honda did a good job of keeping the lid on its plans for a four. Only six weeks before the 1968 Tokyo Show, the UK weekly *Motor Cycle* ran a front page story in which it said it could confirm that Honda was working on a 750cc twin. Then, on the eve of the show in mid-October, the specialist press throughout the world published slightly fuzzy sneak photos of a prototype Honda four under test.

Clearly a development hack carrying various items of test equipment, the machine in the photos could be seen to have an inclined cylinder block, four racer-style megaphone

Four fathers

Belgium's FN company, best known as an armaments maker, put the first viable four-cylinder motorcycle into production in 1904. Designed by Paul Kelecom, it had separate air-cooled cylinders in-line above a crankshaft set longitudinally in the frame, with shaft final drive. Starting out at 362cc it grew to 750cc and survived into the mid-1930s.

Inspired by the FN, the Pierce Arrow four appeared in the United States where similar fours began to proliferate, their makers including Ace, Cleveland, Excelsior X, Henderson and Indian. The last mentioned remained in production until the USA entered the Second World War in 1942, by which time it had undergone considerable modernisation. The smooth-running American fours found favour with police departments and were seen as the ultimate luxury cruisers of their day. Indian four production was not resumed after the war and the factory ceased all production in 1952. In Denmark, the Nimbus longitudinal four was made from 1920 until the 1950s, but few were exported.

Britain came up with the Ariel square four in 1931. Designed by Edward Turner, later prime mover behind Triumph's successful parallel twins, the Ariel 4G had its cylinders in square formation, arranged in pairs on tandem transverse crankshafts linked by gears. A chain took drive to a separate gearbox.

Originally a 500 with an overhead camshaft, the early 4G was much admired, but its launch coincided with the Depression. Subsequent 600cc and 1,000cc versions with pushrod-operated valves continued to be made at the rate of up to 830 per year until 1958. Basically a 1930s design, Ariel's extremely tractable touring engine was liable to become unreliable if ridden hard.

The jaunty image for Ariel's Square four of 1958. (Ariel OC)

silencers finished in black, a fuel tank with chromium-plated side panels and a drum front brake. Confirming that it was a 750, the various reports offered some technical information and most referred to an estimated power output of 80bhp, which was far superior to anything in volume production. Interestingly, some early reports said that the new engine's primary drive was by gears via a countershaft, the system used in Honda's racing multis.

Little more than a week after these photos appeared, the Four made its momentous public Tokyo debut on 25 October. The new model, then named the CB750 Dream Four dominated the Honda stand on a revolving turntable and was the undoubted star of the show. Displayed along with a bare engine, the blue and gold show model was much changed from the test hack in the pre-show photos. But it was still a pre-production machine incorporating various features which would change before the model went on sale. Nevertheless, the general specifications of the CB750 were finalised and its key attractions listed in Honda's press release were as follows:

Four cylinders, four carburettors, four silencers
To provide outstanding performance with rapid acceleration for quick take-offs and overtaking while controlling noise output.

Disc front brake
For strong and reliable braking, yet with feel at the lever.

High-output electrical generator
Ensuring an ample supply of reliable power for all electrical systems.

Double cradle frame
To provide stability at speed.

Sophisticated suspension
Adding stability and giving a high standard of comfort

Specially developed tyres
For sound roadholding without shimmy or patter.

Unlike the Tokyo Motor Show today, which is attended by trade and press representatives from all over the world, events in the 1960s were only reported briefly in the American and European motorcycling press.

However, there were non-Japanese visitors at the 1968 event and they included Joel 'Jody' Nicholas, a top-ranking American road racer then serving in the US Navy as an aircraft pilot. His unit had stopped over at the Yokosuka base en route to a tour of duty in the South China Sea.

'Visiting the Tokyo Show seemed a good way for a group of us in our squadron to develop some memories before entering the Vietnam war.

'The Honda CB750 was mind-boggling to behold. Everything about it seemed just right. The finish of the engine castings, symmetry of the four individual header pipes and mufflers, the chrome plating and the lustrous paint left me spellbound. I knew that when – or if – I got back to America I would have to own one.'

Nicholas would buy his CB750 in April 1970, shortly after being taken on as assistant editor of the monthly *Cycle World* magazine.

Over the winter of 1968-69, Honda geared up to commence production of the Four. Complete machines would be assembled on lines at its Hamamatsu plant, to where completed power units were delivered from the ultra-modern engine factory at Saitama near Tokyo.

Meanwhile, most of the motorcycling world would have to wait anywhere between six and 16 months before getting a close look at a machine that had acquired a fabulous reputation even before anyone had heard it running.

Enter the first superbike

The new Honda was a real eye-catcher, as its designers intended. The Four looked fresh and dynamic without being outlandish. The angular shape of earlier Honda fuel tanks had been abandoned to be replaced by a more traditional and inviting curvaceous form. Yet the metallic-look paintwork and graphics were strikingly modern.

Appropriately, the CB750's unique selling point was its most imposing feature. The four-cylinder power unit filled the frame magnificently, its tilted bank of air-cooled cylinders being obvious from any angle. Using most of the model's chromium plate ration, four prominent exhaust header pipes with grand prix racer-style megaphones spoke of

Dynamic advertising photography helped sell the CB750. Honda chose this view because it showed off the four-pipe exhaust system as well as the Four's generous cornering clearance. (Honda)

potency unprecedented from a standard production roadster.

Features that would be taken for granted today made a big impact when presented on the Honda. Its sheer physical bulk was novel for a Japanese product and the bank of four individual carburettors seemed like sheer extravagance. To eyes accustomed only to drum brakes, the front brake's disc rotor looked huge and the stark clarity of the raised speedometer and rev counter dials was a revelation.

Honda's inspired choice of voguish 'Candy' paint helped the machine turn heads. Developed in the USA, this finish was achieved by applying a carefully measured thickness of transparent tinted lacquer over a bright metallic silver or gold base coat to create a deep and lustrous effect. Since the earliest days of selling the C100 Super Cub, Honda had studied American tastes and fashions in vehicle colour finishes.

Overall the four was a stunning – some would say flashy – package which could hold its own among any gathering of high-status vehicles. The CB750 had sufficient style for cruising fashionable boulevards and promenades from the French Riviera to Southern California. In less glamorous surroundings, it would take over from the custom cafe racer as the top attraction at English bikers' cafes or in queues for the Isle of Man ferry.

The term 'superbike' entered common usage in the early Seventies, to describe the new breed of large-capacity speed machines. Honda can claim to have produced the first of the type, judged on the CB750's lavish specification, high performance and car-type dependability.

Guided tour of the CB750

A landmark engine

Handsome in its aluminium glory on the outside, the CB750 power unit was not internally, as some observers suggested, merely a doubling up of Honda's established sohc twin-cylinder design, but a wholly new engine. Carefully considered with regard to layout, serviceability and manufacture, it represented a landmark for the company and indeed for motorcycle engineering in general.

The unit was based on a main casing consisting of two halves with a horizontal joint passing through the central axes of the crankshaft and the gearbox mainshaft. Held together by 33 hexagon-head bolts, the castings were elaborate in form but neatly shaped on the outside, indicating the sophisticated manufacturing methods of Honda plants in the late 1960s.

Unlike Honda's earlier racing fours, the CB750's crankshaft followed typical car engine practice by featuring plain shell bearings throughout, fed with oil under high pressure. In effect, all metal bearing surfaces were separated by a film of lubricant. A single forging finished by the most up-to-date tooling, the shaft was supported in five main bearings, the substantial housings of which were cast integrally with the main cases. The big-end journals were placed in two up, two down formation so that those of the outer two cylinders reached the top of their strokes when the inner two journals were at bottom dead centre. The bearing journals had a modest diameter of 36mm in order to minimise friction losses.

On the central portion of the shaft, between the webs for the inner two cylinders, three integral chain sprockets were provided for the main output and camshaft drives. Slightly to the right of centre (looking at the unit from the rear), two of the sprockets carried a pair of endless simplex primary chains while a smaller wheel to the left of it, at the shaft's centre, turned an endless chain which drove the camshaft.

Selectively assembled by weight, the forged steel H-section connecting rods and their split-shell big-end bearings were assembled on the journals by caps with two bolts each. Cast aluminium alloy pistons giving a compression ratio of 9:1, a typical figure for a high-performance engine of the time, were carried by gudgeon pins bearing directly in the rods' small-ends. Of sophisticated design, the slightly domed pistons had two compression rings and a third oil scraper ring, treated with a special coating to help initial bedding-in.

A single block cast in aluminium alloy contained the four cylinder bores, each with an iron liner which extended down into the crankcase. To aid cooling, small air passages ran fore and aft between the bores.

Honda GP racers of the 1960s invariably had large-bore, short-stroke, cylinder dimensions for maximum valve area and high rpm, but at 61mm the CB750's bore was 2mm less than its stroke.

This helped minimise overall engine width.

A cavity at the centre of the block enclosed the camshaft drive chain, which was maintained in tension by two jockey wheels bearing on its rear run. A spring-loaded adjuster mounted at the rear of the block casting allowed re-tensioning to be carried out.

The cylinder head was also a single aluminium alloy casting with a central tunnel for the timing chain and two pairs of combustion chambers on either side. Sixteen long studs passing through holes in the block secured it to the top of the crankcase. Early in production, an additional head-to-barrel bolt was added to the front centre of the casting for better gasket sealing.

Operating in conventional guides, the two valves in each chamber were arranged in pairs with an included angle of 60 between them, reflecting the latest trends in combustion chamber design. They were also slightly offset in relation to each other to prevent their heads colliding at high rpm. Valve closing was by conventional double coil springs in inner and outer pairs. A single 12mm sparking plug was located off-centre in each head, placed so as to be accessible for easy removal.

Regional variations

Various features of the CB750 were altered to suit conditions and regulations in different markets. Honda used several particular specifications for Australia, the USA, various individual European countries and other less-specific categories such as General Export and European Direct Sales.

The differences were mostly in lighting systems, switchgear and instrumentation. Headlamp dipping was arranged to suit left- or right-side driving conditions, while rear lamp and indicator types and even lamp bulb ratings varied. Obviously, speedometers had miles-per-hour or kilometres-per-hour calibrations according to the country of sale.

The CB750's detachable silencer baffles varied too, since some markets had stricter noise regulations. More effective diffusers were specified for Germany and the Netherlands, for example, with a consequent slight loss of power output.

An unofficial photograph of a dark green and gold pre-production CB750, taken at the Las Vegas US Honda dealers' convention in January 1969. (World MCs)

On the upper face of the head casting, the one-piece camshaft was carried in four plain shell bearings with detachable caps. The lower bearing mounts were formed by a single cast alloy component bolted to the top of the head, which also held the spindles on which the valve-opening rockers pivoted. It was unusual for Honda, or any other motorcycle engine maker, to opt for plain bearings throughout the engine, but the Four drew on car experience and if high pressure oiling was provided for the bottom end, it made sound engineering sense to use the same system elsewhere.

A single alloy cover enveloping the valve gear and retained by 19 screws had eight inspection covers giving access to individual rocker ends for the adjustment of tappet clearances. A central top cover secured by screws incorporated a breather vent.

The four exhaust ports were recessed to accept bolted-on pipe stubs with gas sealing by copper-asbestos ring gaskets sandwiched between the stubs and the casting. The end of each pipe consisted of an inner and outer tube, fitting over the stub and held in place by a finned clamp.

Each pipe and its silencer was a complete entity, coated in chrome plating. The silencer baffles could be removed for cleaning or de-restriction for competition use, by removing their

Mick Woollett of *Motor Cycle* was the first British journalist to sample the Four at a chilly Brands Hatch circuit, a few days before the Brighton Show in April 1969. (Mick Woollett)

6mm retaining screws. To help muffle noise, short tubes linked each pair of silencers and the rear end of the system was supported by the mounts for the passenger footrests which were located between each pair of silencers. Heat shielding panels fixed to the upper silencers protected the pillion passenger's footwear and ankles.

Carburation was by a bank of four round-slide Keihin PW instruments with venturi tube diameters of 28mm and integral float chambers, held in place by quick-release clips. Their four individual mounts were made of a flexible plastic, deterring heat transfer and absorbing vibration.

Pre-production machines had a cross-shaft and lever operating system linking all four throttles, but for the original CB750 production run another, less-sophisticated, method was employed. Four individual cables led from the throttle slides to a junction box, from where a

Showroom rivals

When the CB750 was released in 1969, several other 750cc motorcycles were being produced in reasonable volume.

BSA and Triumph had announced its new 750s late in 1968. The two makes shared a basically similar 58bhp three-cylinder power unit, outwardly varied to maintain a distinction between the marques. Originally devised in 1963, it was basically a 500cc twin with an added cylinder, retaining vertically split main casings.

Although rather oddly styled, the BSA Rocket 3 and Triumph Trident were exciting performers with a top speed of 125mph. Equipped with four-speed gearboxes, drum brakes and kick-starting, their dry weights were 213kg (470lb) for the BSA and 212kg (468lb) for the Triumph. Poor cornering clearance marred their otherwise sound handling and both had their share of design and assembly flaws.

BSA and Triumph 650cc twins were still going strong, especially the latter, which accounted for a large proportion of the 26,000 Triumphs sold in the USA during 1969.

Norton had been selling 750cc twins since 1962, using an enlarged version of its 500cc engine dating from 1948. The 750 Commando launched in 1968 sought to eliminate vibration, the bugbear of larger parallel-twin engines, using Norton's Isolastic flexible engine mounts. Lively and nimble, the Commando combined big twin character with a relatively smooth ride but Norton did not have the same large following as Triumph in the USA.

The Italian industry took an increased interest in export markets during the late 1960s and Moto Guzzi, the nation's biggest factory, had developed a larger, 757cc ohv V-twin engine for its V7, which was sold in three variants, the 51bhp V7 Special, Ambassador and 750GT California. With an unusual transverse cylinder layout, the Guzzis featured shaft drive, five-speed gearboxes, drum brakes and kick-starting.

Laverda, a smaller Italian firm previously known for its lightweights, had begun to supply small quantities of 750s to America where they were marketed by former Triumph and Honda executive Jack McCormack under the American Eagle badge.

Laverda's 744cc overhead camshaft parallel-twin engine was styled like Honda's CB77 twin, had five speeds and electric starting and offered 115mph (185km/h) performance in 1969. Benelli's contribution to the Italian assault on the bigger bike market was the Tornado 650cc ohv parallel twin.

America's native Harley-Davidson factory in Milwaukee had made motorcycles with large-capacity V-twin engines since before the First World War. Machines of 45cu in (750cc) with side-valve engines were included in the range as medium-sized models from 1930 and this type of engine was still being raced by the factory team in 1969. But that year's road range of H-D motorcycles consisted of 883 and 1,200cc models with ohv V-twin engines. The 883cc four-speed XLH Sportster acquired electric starting from 1968. Weighing over 225kg (496lb), the grunting Harley was claimed to put out 58bhp with a 114mph (183km/h) maximum. The XL Sportster engine had evolved from K Series models first seen more than 15 years earlier.

During 1969, BMW unveiled a new generation of 'boxer' flat twins, indicating that the German factory was gearing up to compete with Japanese products. The largest of its new range was the 745cc R75/5, powered by the latest version of BMW's simple and rugged ohv engine.

It featured shaft final drive, a four-speed gearbox, drum brakes and electric starting. With an output of 55bhp at 6,400rpm, it weighed 190kg (419lb) and was capable of 108mph (174km/h). More of a tourer than a sports bike, the R75/5 was civilised, reliable, and expensive.

Although it only had a capacity of 500cc, Kawasaki's H1 two-stroke triple launched for 1969 had sufficient performance to rank as one of the new breed of superbikes and gain a cult following. Shattering 0-70mph (113km/h) acceleration was off-set by scary handling. Kawasaki Heavy Industries had been a Japanese pioneer in the over-500cc class, marketing its W1 650cc ohv twin from 1966. Then Japan's biggest bike, the W1 had an engine outwardly resembling a 1950s' BSA, and although it enjoyed a following in Japan, it did not sell in large numbers worldwide.

single cable ran to the handlebar twistgrip. The choke control lever for cold starting was mounted on the left instrument and connected to the other carburettors by a linkage.

Honda's determination to equip the Four with a powerful and reliable electrical system was demonstrated by specification of a heavy-duty Hitachi three-phase alternator. Mounted at the leftward end of the crankshaft, it was unusual in employing dc exciter coils to magnetise the rotor rather than the permanent magnets normally found in the rotor of a motorcycle alternator.

Road racer and press tester David Dixon laps the Nürburgring circuit in Germany during the first European press test as organised by *Motorrad* in July 1969. (David Dixon)

Current was generated in another set of ac stator coils arranged around the outside of the rotor, and used to charge the 12-volt, 14-amp-hour battery mounted centrally under the seat. A rectifier converted it to dc and voltage was regulated by an electro-mechanical device, both these units being carried to the left of the battery and easily accessed by removing the left side panel.

At the right-side end of the crankshaft, ignition spark timing was controlled by two sets of contact-breakers activated by a small cam on the shaft. An inspection cover retained by two screws gave rapid accessibility for adjustment, which allowed each cylinder's spark timing to be set individually.

Two ignition coils were concealed under the fuel tank, each having two high-tension leads. One coil sparked the outer cylinders, while the other connected to the plugs of the inner pair.

The transmission layout evidenced designers' efforts to combine mechanical efficiency with compactness and durability, while trying to avoid excess weight. Unlike the CB450, which had primary drive from the crankshaft to its clutch and gearbox by gears, the CB750 used two chains. With only a slight 1.7:1 reduction, they transmitted drive to a duplex sprocket. This was connected via a cush-drive shock absorber containing rubber buffers to the clutch, which contained seven driving and seven driven plates. On very early machines one of the drive plates was attached to the clutch centre. With the clutch engaged, drive was transferred to the gearbox mainshaft and its five constant-mesh pinions.

The layshaft and its pinions were arranged directly below the mainshaft, while a third shaft at

the rear of the unit had a large reduction gear to pick up drive from the layshaft and carried the secondary drive's 16-tooth output sprocket, sited on the left of the unit. The emergency kick-start turned the mainshaft via a pair of gears with a ratchet and pawl mechanism just inboard of the clutch. The larger gear on the kick-start shaft meshed with the oil pump's drive pinions. The gearbox internals were all arranged on the left side of the primary drive line.

The selector-fork gearchange mechanism was operated by a foot lever on the left of the unit, as was normal for Honda. British makers and Harley-Davidson still fitted right-side change pedals at the end of the 1960s, but the left-foot shift was to be standardised by Federal US regulations during the following decade.

Almost all previous Honda power units (some

early GP racers and the 1958 C71 roadster are exceptions) had wet sump lubrication, storing oil in the lower portion of the main cases. But the need to minimise engine height and preserve generous ground clearance led to a dry sump design being adopted for the CB750.

The main reservoir was a frame-mounted tank, linked to the engine by feed and return lines connected to the oil pump. Driven from the transmission, the car-type twin-rotor trochoidal pump was the first of its kind in a Honda motorcycle engine. The pump and a mesh screen used to filter scavenged oil were accessible when a large inspection cover on the underside of the engine was removed.

From the pump's feed side, oil was passed through a relief valve that let off excess pressure at high rpm or when running cold, to the removable filter unit located in cool air flow on the front of the main casing. After being pumped through the filter element, oil was distributed around the power unit via internal plumbing, mostly consisting of galleries within engine components.

Finding its way back to the bottom of the engine by gravity, oil was returned to the tank by the high-capacity scavenge side of the pump, some of it being routed through oilways inside the gearbox shafts so as to lubricate the transmission with engine oil.

A main oil distribution gallery ran transversely in the upper crankcase behind the cylinder block with a removable plug at one end for periodical cleaning-out. A threaded plug at the base of the engine allowed oil in the lower crankcase half to be drained off during changes.

Adopting an idea once used on British AJS racers, lubricant was passed through the transmission output shaft and distributed across the sprocket's inner face to lubricate the final drive chain. Before the advent of modern chains incorporating O-ring seals to retain pre-packed grease, preserving the drive chains of the most powerful machinery could be a problem. During production a rather hit-and-miss method of metering the oil feed was introduced.

A recess behind the left pair of cylinders in the upper main casing contained the starter motor, concealed under a plated cover. It engaged with the crankshaft via a small intermediate pinion, meshing with a large gear situated inboard of the alternator rotor. A free-wheel clutch mechanism between it and the rotor allowed it to remain stationary once the engine had fired and was spinning. The CB750's starter was to prove utterly reliable in service.

Imposing structure

Honda stuck with a conventional, proven format when it came to chassis design. Any radical deviation from the accepted norm for larger, high-performance machines would probably have risked sales resistance. Apart from its disc front brake, the CB750 frame and suspension followed a pattern that had become familiar on more successful racing and road machines and was a distant descendant of the hugely influential Norton 'featherbed' road racing frame of 1950.

It may look spindly and even flimsy compared with today's super-stiff sports bike frames, but the CB750 tubular steel item was perceived as being sturdy in its time, and Honda certainly took pains in attempting to create a structure that could deal with its biggest and most powerful motorcycle engine to date.

Engineers would have been aware that the GP team's most powerful dohc four, the 500cc RC181, had been a notoriously bad handler, thanks to chassis deficiencies.

The CB750's frame surrounded the power unit and was braced for rigidity in the most critical areas, notably behind and below the steering head and around the support points for the rear suspension's swingarm.

Constructed from tube with sheet-steel fillets added to deter twisting, the swingarm acted against a pair of Showa spring and damper units. Made under a de Carbon patent, these were unusual for the time in employing nitrogen gas to prevent aeration in the oil used as a damping medium. The only provision for adjustment was a three-way pre-load setting enabling the owner to stiffen up the springing when carrying a passenger or luggage. Chrome plating on the units' semi-exposed coil springs and dust covers was in tune with the CB750's dashing looks.

Front suspension was by a conventional telescopic fork of the type most commonly found on road and racing motorcycles since BMW had pioneered its use in the 1930s. Containing long coil springs and oil damping valves, the fork had polished aluminium lower sliders and flexible bellows-type gaiters to protect the plated main

The author rides a very low-mileage 1970 model in 1996. This machine belonged to Honda UK before being acquired by road racer Bob Heath. (Jason Critchell)

tubes from grit and water. Ballrace bearings were used in the steering head.

The wheels were the wire-spoked type which were universal on motorcycles of the 1960s, with plated steel rims manufactured by DID. Rim sizes were normal for the bigger bikes of the period, with a large-diameter, 19-inch front wheel and an 18-inch rim at the rear.

Japanese-made Dunlop and Bridgestone tyres were fitted as original equipment, both being a four-ply S-rated type with a ribbed tread for the front. Sizes were 3.25in x 19in front and 4.00 x 18in rear, which look extremely narrow by today's standards.

In the absence of a drum brake, the front hub was a simple 'cotton reel' type in aluminium alloy with a steel carrier bolted to its left side holding the 300mm diameter brake rotor.

Honda's disc brake had a finned caliper with a single live piston set ahead of the left fork leg, carried on an arm which pivoted laterally on a vertical pin. A compression spring and adjuster screw with a locking nut provided a way of setting the caliper's initial alignment. A hydraulic piston pressed the outer pad against the rotor, while the inner pad was brought into contact with the rotor by movement of the arm. The hydraulic system's master cylinder was incorporated into the handlebar brake lever mounting, a neat layout which has become the norm on virtually all motorcycles.

One of the snags facing Honda when developing its disc brake was that the cast iron material found best for braking efficiency and freedom from squeal on cars rapidly rusted when exposed to water. Considering that this would look too unsightly on a motorcycle, engineers found a grade of non-corroding stainless steel that would give satisfactory performance. Vacant caliper mounting lugs on the right side made it possible to add a second disc.

Incorporating a drum brake, the cast-alloy full-width rear hub carried a 45-tooth final drive sprocket with a cush-drive to absorb snatches. A moulded plastic guard reinforced at its central mounts by a steel U-plate shrouded the chain's upper run.

The front and rear mudguards (fenders in US parlance) were broad enough to be effective yet slim enough to look sporting. The front blade was pressed from steel and chrome plated, while the rear item was partly a plastic moulding, with its visible after-section in plated metal.

Holding 16 litres (4.8 US gallons/4 UK gallons), the pressed-steel fuel tank featured a flip-up filler cap, quickly released by pressing a thumb-tab alongside the pivot point at its rear. A plated bead ran along the base, matched by a similar embellishment on the seat and on each side a cast-metal badge, consisting simply of the word 'Honda' was secured by a small spring-steel clip.

Butting up against the rear of the tank, the dual seat had a grab-strap, mandatory in some US states, running over its upper surface and a slightly raised tail end, hinting at the passenger's need for support during sudden acceleration. After releasing a catch, the seat could be hinged up for access to the battery, a kit of tools and an owner's handbook.

Moulded plastic side panels, each featuring a group of six rectangular air-intake slots, were used to enclose the under-seat area. Both had simple mounts with moulded-in tongues press fitting into rubber grommets in frame brackets. Their badges, featuring Honda Wing emblems, had pins on their rear faces which pierced holes in the mouldings and were secured by spring-steel 'speed nuts'. On the right side, the panel concealed the oil tank while removing the left cover revealed the fuse box and other electrical equipment. Lifting the hinged seat gave access to a basic toolkit and the battery, ahead of which was sited the moulded air-filter box connected to the carburettor inlets via flexible adapters.

Engine of change. Honda's revolutionary four-cylinder unit produced the performance required while being compact and economical to manufacture. (Honda)

Early rarities

Many fans of the earliest CB750 are intrigued by the differences between pre-production Fours and the machine that eventually reached the public.

The original Tokyo Show exhibit had side panels that were markedly different from those adopted for production, with integral air-box shrouds and badges based on an elliptical emblem. Masses of minor external details distinguish the earliest pre-production engines which have the word 'Honda' on the cam cover rather than 'OHC 750'. Hand-made, the units contain billet crankshafts machined from the solid. A linking bar was used to operate the carburettor throttle slides.

A later generation of pre-production machines, which appeared at the Las Vegas convention and European shows, had production-style side panels and four-cable throttle operation. However, some small details, would be changed for production, such as a rigid metal pipe running to the front brake master cylinder, which was replaced by a flexible version.

Even customer machines from the first few months of production exhibit seemingly endless small external and internal variations, and some of the components used are almost certainly irreplaceable today.

Lighting differed according to the country of import. The traditional-looking headlamp with its chrome rim and plastic shell contained a Stanley car-type sealed-beam unit as required on US market models, while UK machines had a detachable bulb with moderately powered 50/40-watt filaments for the main and dipped beam respectively. The rear lamp bracket was chromed on US models and finished in black enamel on UK imports.

On earlier twins, Honda had been inclined to set the speedometer, and in the case of the CB450 also the rev-counter, neatly within the headlamp shell. But the 750 had its pair of self-contained instruments set at a 45° angle above the headlamp, enhancing the machine's purposeful appearance as well as making them easier to read at a glance. Supplied by Nippon Denso, the speedo was calibrated to 150mph for the UK and USA or 220km/h for metric markets and its companion tachometer on the right side, ran up to 10,000rpm with a red warning zone from 8,500rpm to 9,300rpm. Both instruments had highly visible orange tips on their white needles which were under slightly domed clear plastic lenses.

Warning lights were incorporated in the instrument dials, with the main beam indicator and direction indicator repeater on the speedometer with a neutral indicator and oil warning light in the rev-counter. At night, internal lighting gave them an eerie, but attractive glow.

Western-style handlebars, fitted to suit American tastes, carried switch clusters adjacent to each hand grip, the lighting and engine kill-switch controls being built neatly into the throttle drum on the right, where the starter button was also located.

The key-operated ignition switch was located below the forward part of the fuel tank on the left. Direction indicators, which Honda had fitted to the Cub step-thrus since 1958, were included in the CB750's luxury package. Mounts for the front pair were combined with the headlamp fixings and the rear indicators carried on the rearmost part of the frame. Side-facing orange reflectors were mounted on the headlamp support brackets to comply with US safety regulations.

At first the colour options were Candy Blue-Green or Candy Red, but Candy Gold was soon available too. The coloured components were the fuel tank, which had a contrasting gold flash outlined with pin-stripes sweeping along the upper surface each side, the headlamp shell and its brackets, the side panel mouldings and the visible portion of the air box.

The CB750 was featured on the cover of the US magazine *Cycle World* for January 1969, and four machines were unveiled by Soichiro Honda himself at that month's Las Vegas dealer convention marking Honda's 10 years in North America and the sale of one million motorcycles in that market. Testing of pre-production machines in American conditions had been conducted in the somewhat sparsely populated state of Nevada.

Although the official date for releasing the CB750 in North America was early in June, the first shipment of production models had left Japan for American Honda's base at Gardena, California in April to reach US and Canadian dealers' showrooms in May.

Honda really went to town in producing attractive up-to-date publicity material of the highest quality to promote the CB750. Before the Four arrived in the USA, awareness was built up by a four-page colour brochure stapled into national magazines. It was headed by the slogan 'Sooner or later, you knew Honda would do it'. The front and back pages carried action shots of a rider in bright clothing and wearing the latest type of visor windshield with an open-face helmet. His machine is a pre-production

type with detail differences from the customer machine.

Inside was a double-page spread showing the Honda in US market production form and punchy text concluding with the warning: 'When you twist the throttle, remember one thing. You asked for it.'

In June 1969 a more elaborate brochure was issued, which unfolded into a 630 x 300mm poster of a Candy Blue-Green CB750 shot against a black background. The text above it simply read: 'Honda CB750 Four . . . 4 cylinders

. . . 5 speeds . . . 125mph . . . 12.6sec ¼ mile . . . Disc brake'. There were also dynamic images accentuating the engine, the four exhaust pipes and clear instrumentation. Including a photograph of a woman at the controls was a progressive move, although there were also traditional shots of models posing with a static machine. The Japanese language CB750 brochure was a lavish production with no less than 12 pages!

These publications may look unremarkable against the plethora of sophisticated makers' publicity that bombards us today, but in 1969 they were at the cutting edge of motorcycle advertising. Helped by favourable press tests and the shrewd pricing policy that undercut BSA and Triumph 750s, the sophisticated marketing helped achieve good sales in the CB750's launch year. In June, it was claimed that 5,000 Fours had been manufactured and shipped to USA and Canada, with output from Hamamatsu running at 2,000 units a month. Numbers like that really blew the British competition into the weeds. Don Brown, a US market analyst who was sales chief at BSA Inc's New Jersey HQ in 1969, recalled: 'From the time Honda announced the CB750 Four with its slim British look, electric starter, extra cylinder and all at a cheap price, the game was all but over for us. Sales of our triple were very disappointing.

'But while the Honda Four spelled the end of the once-mighty BSA Group, its demise was really the inevitable result of 10 years of complacency on the part of British manufacturers. Their old-world financiers and labour unions remained blind to the Japanese threat. Numerous attempts to modernise plant and equipment were blocked, and talented designers were prevented from introducing modern designs at key market prices. You could say the British industry had already died by the time the CB750 arrived in the States.'

Landing in Europe

The first sighting of the new Four in Europe was in Holland early in February 1969. A pre-production machine was flown over by Honda Motor Imports of Eindhoven, who showed it to Dutch dealers. Under strict orders not to start the engine, importer Tom Riemersma was unable to quote a price but anticipated receiving his first consignment in August.

Days later, a CB750, possibly the same machine, was in Britain. It was featured in a piece on motorcycling for the BBC TV motoring programme *Wheelbase* filmed on Lord Montagu's estate at Beaulieu in Hampshire. The Four was fired up and demonstrated, when Honda UK service chief and former road racer Alf Briggs performed rear wheel spinning getaways for the cameras.

In March, the Honda was presented to the French motorcycle press and invited VIPs by Honda France staff including a factory representative, at the exclusive Pré de Catalan restaurant in the Bois de Boulogne district of Paris.

Two pre-production Fours, one green and the other gold, were revealed 'in the flesh' to the British public at the country's main show of 1969 held in early April at the Metropole Exhibition Centre in the seaside resort of Brighton. Prior to the show, a machine had been presented to the press at a reception held in London's Charing Cross Hotel, allowing monthly publications to obtain details and photos in advance.

The claimed power had now been nudged down to 70bhp and it was suggested that an initial batch of only 12 machines would come to Britain, with approximately 100 per year subsequently imported for sale through selected dealers.

Mick Woollett, sports editor of *Motor Cycle*, was the first UK journalist to ride a Four, at the Brands Hatch racing circuit, a few days before the Brighton show opened. Admitting he had ridden gingerly rather than risk damaging the precious display model, he only offered general impressions in a short quarter-page piece in the Show issue of the tabloid weekly.

Describing the machine as 'delightfully smooth and comfortable', Woollett said it gave the impression of being more a luxury tourer than an out-and-out sports model.

Forged, plain-bearing crankshaft with integral drive sprockets. (John Colley)

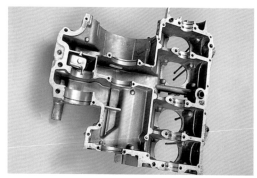

Single casting that forms upper half of main power unit casing. (John Colley)

Spigot and compression flange ensures effective sealing of exhaust pipe at port. (John Colley)

Stator, rotor and field coil (top) of 180W Hitachi alternator. (John Colley)

Frame with well-braced steering head. This type is post-1971. (John Colley)

The tank design is a happy blend of modern and traditional styling. (John Colley)

Flip-up fuel filler cap with a thumb latch to one side, at the rear. (John Colley)

Praising the five-speed transmission highly for its slick changes, he was less enthusiastic about the front brake, speculating that it probably needed bedding-in to give its best. Calling the CB750 a 'two-wheeled status symbol', Woollett joined other UK commentators who perceived the new four as an exclusive flagship rather than a mass seller.

Honda was still a relatively small operation in Britain and several members of the Honda Owners Club, founded by Mike Evans in 1961, were brought in by Honda UK boss Jim Harrisson to help staff the show stand.

The green Four on display was raised on a special stand above head-level over a map of the Isle of Man TT course, evoking Honda's TT racing record, while the gold-painted machine was at ground level. The CB750 Four aimed to steal the show, especially since the Honda stand was adjacent to the combined BSA and Triumph display. A signboard said: 'Look around the Honda CB750, there's nothing to compare with it.'

The British combine was showing its three-cylinder 750cc BSA Rocket 3 and Triumph Trident, announced seven months earlier as export-only models. They were now to be released on the home market, and were being seen for the first time by most showgoers.

Honda announced the CB750's UK price at Brighton, which at £650 made it the most expensive bike on display and a couple of weeks' wages costlier than the triples. BSA and Triumph staff, reeling from news

earlier in the year that the Honda would significantly undercut the triples in the USA, were relieved.

But when the British 750s' specifications were directly compared with the Honda's they could not match it. Their power output was 59bhp against the 67bhp now claimed for the Four and they did not offer electric starting, a five-speed gearbox or a disc brake. Other disadvantages of the British 750s were their lack of direction indicators, no rear-view mirrors fitted as standard and ironically, rather angular styling that many BSA and Triumph fans considered 'too Japanese'.

Nevertheless, Honda UK had been sufficiently stung by the disappointing sales of the CB450 to remain cautious about the CB750's sales prospects. It was probably because no large orders had been placed with the factory that no Fours arrived for British customers until the following year.

However, Cheshire dealer and road racer Bill Smith, who had forged links with Honda from the company's first TT visits, soon had a machine for evaluation which he took to the Isle of Man TT race meeting in June 1969.

Some UK customers were clamouring for a Four, but they had to wait until early 1970 to get their dream machine. The first batch, believed to be no more than 24 and all sold before they landed in England, arrived at the end of January and several bigger consignments followed in the following months. The list price had crept up to £680.

After being put on public display at the

Left side panel moulding with six air slots and hexagonal badge. (John Colley)

The kick-start lever provides reassurance, but is seldom needed. (John Colley)

Instruments are tilted and raised for quick and easy reading. (John Colley)

A heat shield on the upper silencer protects passenger's footwear. (John Colley)

The finned front brake caliper is carried on an adjustable mounting arm. (John Colley)

The black-enamelled tail light assembly, as fitted for the UK market. (John Colley)

French Grand Prix held on the Le Mans circuit in May, the Four would go on sale in France during August and was destined to play a major role in the huge upsurge of interest in motorcycling which occurred throughout that country during the 1970s. The nickname it acquired, *Quattre Pattes*, which translates as 'four-legs', confirmed its French status as the definitive four-cylinder motorcycle.

Early in 2000, more than 30 years after the Le Mans launch, a readers' poll in the French monthly *Moto Legende* voted the CB750

This Candy Ruby Red machine has a chrome-plated tail lamp assembly specified for markets other than the UK, Germany and the Netherlands. (Honda)

'Motorcycle of the 20th Century' by a clear majority. The magazine summed up the CB750's historic importance succinctly: 'Just as Christendom measures time by reference to the birth of Jesus Christ, the motorcycling world is clearly divided into two epochs: before and after the appearance of the *Quattre Pattes*.'

More than 500 Fours had been sold in France by the end of 1969. Honda sales generally increased by a staggering 15 times in France from the 751 machines of over 51cc registered in 1968 to 11,629 by 1971. Much of this dramatic increase could be ascribed to sales of the

CB750 itself and its positive influence on the two-wheeled scene as a whole. By 1978, the total sales of the CB750 and its derivatives in France would exceed 22,000.

In Sweden, the Honda importer Auto Hansa obtained a CB750 to show off at an international race meeting held on the Scandinavian Raceway at Anderstorp in August 1969. Bo Granath, one of Sweden's leading road racers, rode the machine in a one-hour production machine event. Being in completely standard trim it was not very competitive against specially prepared entries, but finished in ninth place behind the dominant Triumph twins and a Kawasaki triple.

As happened in France, the CB750's arrival coincided with a motorcycling boom, helped when Sweden liberalised its learner machine laws in 1970s, effectively allowing young novice riders to learn on Japanese 125s. Although the country's climate restricts road riding to the months from May until October, there are many miles of uncrowded roads.

In 1969, there was no upper speed limit on major routes. The good times, which peaked in 1982, would see 22,000 machines a year sold in Sweden, against today's average of under 15,000.

Deliveries to Australia, a country with a strong motorcycling heritage where riders enjoy year-round good riding weather, started in July and competitive pricing saw machines being snapped up as soon as they reached the dealers. Honda Australia had only been established a few months earlier .

The CB750's release to the buying public in its native country was delayed by a long wait for approval by the Japanese transport ministry, which had been concerned to learn of the new bike's 120mph (193km/h) top speed. This actually served as excellent free publicity, helping to make the Four a hot seller when finally put on sale in Japan during August 1969. The Honda was also soon adopted as a fleet machine by the Presidential Police. For some years, 750cc was set as the maximum capacity for motorcycles sold in Japan.

Back in April 1969, a riding launch had been laid on for the home press at the Arakawa test circuit, previously used for track development of Honda grand prix racing machines. For the first time at such an event, the company laid on full medical facilities including doctors, nurses and stretchers. It was feared that some of the Japanese journalists might come to grief on a machine that was much bigger and heavier than

any Honda before it. But, according to Honda, even testers standing shorter than 1.7m (5ft 6in) reported that once under way the CB750 was as easy to ride as a Super Cub.

In Germany, the fortnightly *Motorrad* organised the first proper European test rides on the Honda at the Nürburgring race circuit in July, taking along a Münch Mammoth for comparison. Selling against the newly announced 750cc BMW twin, Honda's German HQ sold 500 CB750s in the model's first year of availability.

Displayed among the wide variety of home products at the 1969 Milan show, the Four created a stir but would not reach the Italian market until early 1970. An analysis of the CB750 published by November's *Motociclismo* said that the Four demonstrated the Japanese philosophy of confronting European makers with machines of superior performance and technology. It questioned why, if Kawasaki's 500 triple produced 60bhp, the Honda only made 67. After all, it reasoned, had there had not been reports from Japan late in 1968 suggesting that the Four would deliver over 70bhp? The writer suggested that power output may have been backed off to achieve the civility, comfort and flexibility of a Gran Turismo model, rather than aiming at a grand prix racer for the street. Also, the possibility that Honda was unable to tame a more potent engine with its available frame technology was raised.

As the four-cylinder engine was so much bigger and more complex than other motorcycle units of the time, it could have presented a headache to dealers' workshop staff. But, according to Mick Wood, who worked on CB750s as a mechanic at the English Midlands Honda dealer Devimead, the CB750 unit held no terrors for a skilled practitioner: 'Servicing was basically the same as on other bikes, except that there was more of everything, which wasn't a problem. The single overhead cam layout was very easy to work on compared with the shimming-up required on later double overhead cam heads. It was a really lovely motor to work on – better than many more modern fours in that respect.'

There were teething troubles with the early CB750, and perhaps they were the inevitable result of a high-speed development programme. Problems included drive-chain breakages, head joint leaks, charging system failures and porous castings, but all were addressed through Honda's warranty system and multifarious changes were made in production in order to address known weaknesses.

The sceptics

Naturally, the new Honda did not find favour with everyone. Committed 'scratchers' found it top-heavy and more cumbersome than typical European sport machines over twisting and mountainous roads.

Some sceptics expected the engine to prove fragile, especially in view of the plain-bearing crankshaft, although over the long term the CB750's car-like dependability became legendary and proved them wrong. Owners used to carrying out all their own routine maintenance were shocked at the Honda's apparent complexity. Also, they were not comforted by the fact that the whole unit had to be taken out of the frame before the rocker cover could be lifted.

Motorcyclists accustomed to changing worn primary chains on British twins before Sunday brunch, were concerned at the thought of two chains buried deep within the Honda's bottom end. Nor could they tweak the carburation satisfactorily with a screwdriver and a couple of small spanners: the CB750's four instruments could only be dialled-in properly with a set of vacuum gauges.

But, of course, the Honda could cover high mileages at speed with minimal need for attention, unlike some of its contemporaries.

In Britain and the USA there was an element of motorcyclists who were simply anti-Japanese.

They derided the CB750 for being flashy and too much like a two-wheeled car.

Ironically, they criticised what they saw as cheap finish at a time when British and American manufacturers were getting into serious difficulties with their quality control.

The same detractors were likely to be busy on maintenance and repair chores when their CB750-mounted peers were out on the road and burning up the miles.

To some extent, Honda did build down to a price. Areas not visible on the completed machine were not polished and Japanese frame welding was notoriously messy, although there was no evidence to suggest that it lacked structural strength. Some compromise had resulted in a machine of superior specification which was not the exclusive preserve of the super-rich, but priced to be affordable to ordinary working people.

Put to the test

Not surprisingly, given its revolutionary specification, the CB750 received almost universal acclaim in press road tests. Some of the earliest articles were really just impressions of what it was like for a road rider to get to grips with such a novel and exciting motorcycle, based on a brief loan of a demonstrator machine. But more thorough tests were to follow, setting out the hard facts that potential buyers and hopeful dreamers alike wanted to know.

American Honda must have been heartened to read one of the first US riding impressions: 'Although produced in Japan, the 750 is an American motorcycle. It's big, it's fast and its flashy,' enthused *Cycle Guide* in March 1969, under its headline The Ultimate. Remarking on the Honda's obvious size and weight, the piece went on to say that its bulk was not a problem once on the move, and that the machine was manageable in heavy traffic as well as being quite comfortable when bowling along at speed on a freeway. Praising the decision to opt for a high-revving multi-cylinder engine, *Cycle Guide* really liked the howling exhaust note, comparing it to sounds of the Isle of Man TT races.

Another feature of the Four that found favour was its tidy and efficient linked cross-shaft throttle mechanism, but ironically this would be absent from customer machines until being introduced as standard during 1970. Bikes released to the American press for early impressions were the pre-production versions, which differed in several minor respects from customer machines about to fill the showrooms.

The magazine reported that it did not have the machine long enough for performance testing to be carried out, but predicted a 125mph (200km/h) top speed and rather optimistically quoted power output at 75bhp.

Rival monthly *Cycle World*, which had featured a pre-production version on its cover in January 1969, published an exhaustive road test in its August issue. The performance figures were not disappointing: top speed was given as 123.24mph (198.29km/h) and the standing quarter-mile covered in 13.38 seconds with a terminal speed of over 100mph (in fact, 100.11mph/161.08km/h). The writer pointed out that the engine was actually in a mild state of tune, helping to achieve its surprising degree of flexibility. Fuel consumption was quoted at 35mpg US (equivalent to 42mpg UK/6.74-litre/100km), sinking below 30mpg (36mpg UK/7.86-litre/100km) during a six-hour stint of aggressive road riding at speeds of up to 110mph (177km/h).

Points singled out for particular praise were the power and feel of the disc brake, unexpectedly generous cornering clearance and the attractive, easy-to-read instruments. CW found both the front and rear suspension were rather firm but even so, called the Honda the finest handling machine in its weight class.

A top speed of 131mph (211km/h) quoted in *Cycle*'s full road test of the same month was probably a speedometer reading rather than an accurate timed figure. But its standing-start quarter-mile figures were almost identical to that of a rival publication. *Cycle*'s writer journeyed around California on the test Honda in company with a 500cc Kawasaki triple. He reported that the two-stroke was clearly faster accelerating up to 90mph, but at that point the Honda stormed away from the smaller machine. The Four was complemented on its handling over twisting unfamiliar roads and the tester described an exciting high-speed blast on deserted roads at night. The sealed-beam headlamp fitted to the North American CB750 proved effective and the disc brake was applauded for its power, although it needed a hard pull on the hand lever to get the best from it. The writer reported locking the rear wheel when braking very hard.

The Honda's roadholding and suspension got a clear thumbs-up, even though these aspects of the Four would eventually be seen as its weaker points as riders became used to the strong performance.

It seems very strange today, but *Cycle*'s 1969 tester admitted to being wary of the Honda's direction indicators, which he viewed as a dubious novelty. However, after riding on busy roads he was convinced that they helped to keep cars at bay. The few criticisms related to difficulty in heaving the weighty machine on to its centre stand and the mess created when the drive chain flung its oil on to parts of the machine and eventually the garage floor. Honda would address this common complaint by elongating the chainguard during the CB750's production run.

Motorrad ran its test early in August, having conducted it at the tortuous 14.2-mile (23km) Nürburgring circuit with seasoned journalist Ernst Leverkus, who wrote under the 'Klacks' byline. He had collaborated with instrument maker

Kienzle to devise a tachograph that would operate off a motorcycle's speedometer cable. The resulting print-out showed speeds at all points of the circuit and provided useful comparisons between machines in *Motorrad*'s extremely thorough tests. Leverkus commented: 'Here we have a very, very fast motorcycle which handles well and enables deceptively high speeds to be maintained. You are often going faster than you realise, which could be a danger for inexperienced riders. At a steady 140–160km/h (85-95mph) autobahn speed no vibration can be felt and there is still a lot of power to come.'

'It's a Gran Turismo' proclaimed the Australian monthly *Two Wheels* in its September 1969 issue. A full technical description of the CB750 was run with riding impressions by the magazine's Japanese correspondent Jack Yamaguchi, since no machines had been available in Australia by press time. He rode it up to 110mph, in an inappropriate rally jacket, on the Honda test track since the Four was unlicensed, awaiting its official release on the home market.

The British weekly *Motor Cycle* published its first comprehensive UK-based road test in April 1970 as part of a 16-page Honda promotional supplement. The tester was seasoned professional David Dixon, who had already sampled the Four on overseas circuits in the previous year, including the Nürburgring, where his publication had been invited to join *Motorrad*'s test days. His main observation was how effectively the 750 concealed an iron fist in a velvet glove. The standing start quarter mile was covered in a scorching 12.6 seconds, the best time by any machine in a *Motor Cycle* road test, and yet the machine was found to be commendably flexible and docile at low speeds. A top speed of 121mph was recorded in a one-way run with a tailwind, and Dixon remarked that his cruising speed was dictated not by the

Honda's power or handling but by wind-blast discomfort caused by the high handlebars.

While Dixon found he could rev the engine freely to 8,500rpm, he reported that using a mere 5,000rpm was enough to 'see off virtually anything on the road'.

As some owners were to discover, changing to a lower handlebar bend for speed riding was not a simple matter because internally routed electrical wiring, control cables and the front brake hose were all tailor-made to the existing 'high bars' set-up.

The Four was commended for a well-balanced feel that made its bulk immaterial on the move, although Dixon noted rather heavy steering at low speed. A tendency to 'fall-in' to slow corners was to become a generally acknowledged attribute of the CB750 throughout its production life. Riding on Japanese Dunlops, Dixon said they were equal to their British made equivalents on dry roads but inferior in the wet. Again, this conclusion was to be borne out by many owners' experiences.

Easy starting and remarkable smoothness marred only by patches of mirror-blurring vibration were other plus features pointed out by a tester with extensive experience of British high-performance machines that vibrated to the point of discomfort, and sometimes needed several hefty swings of the kickstart to be fired up.

General comfort on the CB750 was highly rated: the seat was said to be comfortable even after 300 miles (480km) were covered in a day.

Recalling his time with the Candy Gold-coloured UK press machine, YLY 70H (which survives today in private hands), Dixon told the author that although the CB750 came, over time, to be criticised for handling flaws, it very much impressed him with its stability on first acquaintance.

'I had a cross-country route that took me from my home in Surrey to the MIRA (Motor Industry Research Association) testing grounds in

ooner or later, you knew Honda would do it.

Front page of the brochure inserted in American magazines
early in 1969.

Warwickshire (a journey of about 125 miles). Doing it on the Honda was a revelation. It was phenomenally quick off the mark and rode really well on the variety of roads included in the route. Its outstanding features were power, good braking and fantastic smoothness. Looking back, another thing that really impressed me at the time was that in three separate tests I did in Germany, Sweden and Britain, the speed figures came up almost exactly the same. That was a kind of consistency that the British factories had never been able to achieve and it showed how advanced Honda was with production technology. It was also great to be able to ride high mileages at speed without needing to carry odd tools, fuses and bits of wire for making running repairs.'

Motorcycle Mechanics was loaned YLY 70H and in its June 1969 issue, editor Charles Deane enthused about the 'fastest accelerating roadster ever tested', reporting a 12.4-second standing quarter-mile and a 125mph (200km/h) maximum, with 110–115mph (177–185km/h) possible sitting comfortably upright. Commenting favourably on a surprisingly broad power band he also liked the deeply padded seat and total absence of oil leaks, barring the controlled supply to the rear chain. Less admired were a noisy gearchange, uncertain tyre behaviour in the wet and some 'heart-stopping twitches' if power was poured on while taking bumpy bends at 80mph. Deane also found that the rear wheel locked too easily when braking on wet and greasy London streets.

In a 1970 test, Peter Strong of the weekly *Motor Cycle News* said that the Four's turbine-like acceleration was smooth and effortless but warned that high-speed handling was an art that needed to be mastered and that respect had to be shown in wet weather. He reported wearing out the rear tyre in only 3,500 miles (5,600km), an alarmingly short period by 1970 standards.

Italy's *Motociclismo* tested the CB750 in the spring of 1970. In a detailed and critical test, Guido Rosani said that the Honda was a great motorcycle and not only in its dimensions. He found the machine very stable at speed in a straight line, even in windy conditions and found it behaved well in corners, particularly if they were taken with the throttle held on. Finding 7,000rpm enough for most conditions, he reported spinning the back wheel in second and third gears if 9,000rpm was used. Top speed was calculated at 195km/h (122mph) with the rider crouched but the writer thought that with a better handlebar shape 200km/h (124mph) would be possible. Suggesting that the seating space was generous enough for three people, if such a thing was permitted, he didn't like the US-style riding position: 'It is annoying to ride a motorcycle with such high performance and yet not be able to exceed 140km/h (87mph). Above that speed it becomes impossible to breathe because of the wind on your chest. A more normal handlebar would be preferable: we don't believe that the type of bar fitted is needed to retain complete control.'

Rosani offered an alternative view on several aspects of the CB750. He thought the paintwork attractive but too vulnerable to accidental scratches and opined that the gold tank stripes were in dubious taste. Of the exhaust note he said: 'It is quite subdued and not annoying, even if in absolute terms we can classify it as an ugly sound for a motorcycle. The sound is more like a car.' An unexpected comment from the land that created the original yowling GP fours!

As production continued, of course, more market rivals appeared and the Four's relative shortcomings were revealed, and so reviews naturally tended to become more critical. The CB750 set high standards by which it, in turn, came to be judged.

Evolution by numbers

During the CB750's remarkably long, 10-year production life there were countless minor revisions to its specification and a series of major model updates. Some changes were in response to faults that showed up in use, many were forced on Honda by legislative or safety considerations and others were introduced purely to ensure that the company could be seen to offer something new in an increasingly competitive market as the years rolled by. The CB750-derived Super Sport and Hondamatic models were also introduced in the late Seventies, which are covered in subsequent chapters.

Introduced late in 1970, the K1 has altered badging, side panels without slots and new, black air box. (Honda)

The very earliest production CB750s are distinguished by their 'sand-cast' main engine casings which have a noticeably coarse surface texture like that produced by a sand-casting technique, although they were in fact produced by gravity die casting. Re-tooling at Honda in the face of the tremendous demand for the Four resulted in engines after serial number 1007414 having a much smoother casting produced by a high-pressure die-casting process.

Most of the so-called sand-cast production machines were shipped to North America, but some were also imported to France and Germany. With less than 7,500 having been built, this version is now comparatively rare and especially prized among CB750 collectors.

In recent years, several of these early machines have been dispersed around the world. The very earliest models also had a smoothly finished oil filter housing, but dealers usually replaced it during routine servicing with the much stronger finned type, which superseded it.

Perhaps not surprisingly, in view of the speed with which Honda designed and developed the Four, a number of dealer recall modifications were made in the first year of production. A notable problem that plagued early machines was breakage of the final drive chain, which often destroyed the plastic chainguard and usually caused serious damage to the main engine casings. In response to this weakness, the power unit's 16-tooth output sprocket was enlarged to a 17-tooth size to ease stress on the chain. A small sprocket promotes too extreme a cyclic variation in chain movement.

The first complete update was made to machines released from the autumn of 1970 to which Honda applied the K1 suffix. K stands for a Japanese word written in Roman script as Kariyo, meaning an improvement. Also applied to other Honda models of the period, K1, K2, K3 and so on are similar to MkI, MkII, MkIII

designations sometimes applied by vehicle makers. By chance the numbers mostly correspond to the last digits of their model years, although not necessarily to their dates of actual manufacture. New models were usually launched at shows during the autumn.

The early edition of the Four that preceded the K1 is often labelled as the CB750 K0. This convenient way of distinguishing it from later K-coded machines probably dates from the 1980s. This practice is not accepted by some historians who believe that the earliest machines are correctly referred to simply as the CB750 and they apply the K0 code to a small batch of machines assembled sometime between June and August 1970.

An official Honda dealer publication entitled *Which Model?* distributed in the UK during the early 1970s refers to this transitional model as the CB750 K0, saying that 36 ended up in the UK. A total of 121 were made in this guise, which followed the specification of the 1969-70 CB750 but incorporated the revised throttle operation that was part of the K1 update. The single-cable twistgrip and four-way junction taking a cable to each carburettor was replaced by a rocking beam throttle opening mechanism above the carburettors and a twin-cable push-pull system at the grip. No specific handbook or parts book was issued for this version.

Today's restorers should note that Honda made dozens of piecemeal alterations which do not correspond exactly with code changes. For example, while the majority of K1s have a cylinder block die-casting with straight-edged finning on each flank, some early examples retained the earlier CB750 casting with slight bulging of the fin profiles.

The K1, released in America from September 1970 and available in Europe several weeks later, was to be the biggest seller of the whole K series. It introduced new colour schemes, offering brown (Candy Garnet), green (Valley

Green) and blue (Polynesian Blue Metallic) as well as the existing options. But other obvious changes were made for functional reasons. The side panels and oil tank and seat were now re-shaped in response to criticism of the earlier types, which caused discomfort to some riders, especially those of shorter stature. The new side panel mouldings dispensed with the air slots of the earlier type and carried redesigned badges and '750 Four' lettering.

A very necessary change was made to the air-filter assembly. The original moulded box often developed cracks so it was replaced by a revised item, with vertical ribs and finished in black. Another weakness revealed in use was the vulnerability of the acrylic lenses on the speedometer and rev-counter to spilled brake fluid and other damage, which led to them being replaced by glass covers. At the same time, metal outer casings were adopted for the instruments, which were now sealed and non-serviceable. Clutch rattle was addressed during K1 production by welding a strengthening ring around the clutch basket.

Follow-up fours

Power with agility

Honda's second roadster four, the half-litre CB500, arrived during 1971. Lighter, lower, smoother and less costly than the CB750, the smaller machine could exceed 110mph (177km/h) and offered fine handling. Of a generally similar format to the 750cc engine, but with upright cylinders, the 498cc unit also featured a single overhead camshaft, a five-speed gearbox and electric starting. Primary drive was now by a Morse-patented Hy-Vo inverted-tooth chain, a successor to the Coventry Silent type seen on some British motorcycles of the Twenties. The CB500's styling was easy on the eye and conservative, although the shape of its silencers hinted at US customs. It evolved into the CB550K from 1973.

Sweet middleweight

In mid-1972, the 500 was joined by a CB350 Four. Originally, Honda had planned to produce 'mini fours' in both 250 and 350cc sizes, but abandoned the quarter-litre version, apparently because internal friction losses resulted in disappointing power delivery. The 350cc category was the traditional entry level for young American motorcyclists and Honda had already cornered it with the 305cc Super Hawk and its 1968 successor, the mass-selling 325cc CB350 twin. A sweet-running, comfortable, well-braked machine, which Soichiro Honda said he particularly enjoyed riding, the 347cc Four made a modest 34bhp at 9,500rpm. That was 2bhp less than the 1972 CB350 twin's output, so Honda UK opted not to sell it, but the CB350 Four sold in modest numbers elsewhere in Europe.

The CB750's smaller brothers: CB500 Four, 1972 . . .

Euro-style classic

The CB350 Four was supplanted by the livelier CB400F Super Sport of 1975-78. Assuming almost immediate classic status, the 408cc (399cc in Japan) middleweight had the lean and functional looks of a European-style cafe racer, enhanced by plain but bright colour schemes and an attractive serpentine four-into-one exhaust system. Compact, easy to handle and reasonably fleet, the 'Four-hundred Four' appealed to sporting riders in Europe who like to dash around snaking byways rather than drum along for long distances on US-style highways. Its market success and enduring

. . . and CB350 Four of the same year. (Honda)

popularity in the UK was reflected when Britain's Honda Owners Club held a CB400F 20th anniversary rally in 1995 which was attended by no fewer than 300 examples.

A similarly styled CB550F Super Sport arrived for 1975, followed in turn by the less elegant CB650, which with the demise of the CB750, became the largest capacity Honda to be powered by a sohc in-line four engine. It was marketed until early 1984, acquiring the Nighthawk model name with appropriate dark livery from 1982. Less than predatory in character, the 650 had its strongest following in the USA.

Fours to the fore

Since the mid-1970s, Honda has offered countless overhead camshaft fours from 250 to 1,300cc. Although the company adopted the V-twin and V4 engine formats for sportsters, tourers and cruisers during the early 1980s, the continuity of the Honda transverse in-line fours was assured by the launch of the successful CBR series in 1987. The speedy yet versatile CBR600F Super Sport has been one of Honda's best sellers and the edgy, lightweight CBR900RR FireBlade launched in 1992 became a legend in its own production life.

Nimble and attractive, the CB400F Super Sport of 1975. (Honda)

The K2 has its warning lights in a fascia on the upper handlebar clamp. (John Colley)

The lower button on the left console mutes the K2's indicator buzzer. (John Colley)

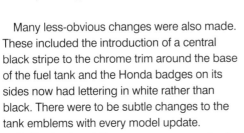

The jumbo rear light unit with side reflectors for the US market. (John Colley)

Honda lettering on the engine covers is now on a black background. (John Colley)

Many less-obvious changes were also made. These included the introduction of a central black stripe to the chrome trim around the base of the fuel tank and the Honda badges on its sides now had lettering in white rather than black. There were to be subtle changes to the tank emblems with every model update.

On the front end, there was a narrower front wheel hub with an altered brake rotor with speedometer drive box to suit, and subtle changes to the fork sliders. The front mudguard's plain front and rear edges were given rolled lips: the sharp leading edge had always threatened to act as a 'pedestrian slicer'. An anti-corrosion coating on the brake caliper changed its colour from silver to black.

The flat-topped seat. Cover patterns were constantly revised. (John Colley)

The anti-jam plate on the outer face of the rear sprocket, for safety. (John Colley)

The K2's oil-damped shock looks similar to the earlier de Carbon type. (John Colley)

The US tyre and loading information sticker on the rear mudguard. (John Colley)

The first of many changes were made to the rear suspension units, providing slightly stouter coil springs with top and bottom anti-chafe seatings. The rear wheel sprocket grew to a 48-tooth size, used in conjunction with an 18-tooth item on the transmission output shaft. The rear hub cush drive was also revised, altering the relative sizes of the rubber inserts. An alternative, lower, handlebar bend was specified for the European-market K1s since many riders found the high American style uncomfortable for sustained high-speed cruising. The K1 seat was slimmer at the front and dispensed with the sporty raised ledge at the rear.

In summary, the K1 offered improved comfort and dependability while retaining the character

and performance of the original CB750. Its
quoted weight was 235kg (518kg), 17kg (37lb)
heavier than the first version.

   Now that the Four was no longer a novelty,
press tests were a little more critical. *Cycle
Guide*'s Bob Braverman suggested that better
tyres were needed to prevent a wriggle on
some road surfaces. He complained of jerky
throttle response at low speeds and objected
to the heavy operation of the centre stand.
Overall, though, the test confirmed that the
Honda was master of its class with robust and

tireless performance at speeds over 70mph
(112km/h). It was also praised for flexibility,
generous cornering clearance and a
transmission that performed faultlessly despite
harsh treatment in speed testing. The exhaust
sound was still seductive: Braverman called it
'out of sight'.

   Sales were really taking off by 1971 with an
estimated 77,000 of the K1 type distributed
worldwide before the 1972 update arrived.

   A whole new range of colours was introduced
for the K2, when it was released early in 1972.

Peer group placings

The Italian monthly Motociclismo set up a comparison test between six current 750cc superbikes in 1972. They were a Honda CB750 K2, a Ducati GT V-twin, Kawasaki H2 triple, Laverda SF parallel-twin, Moto Guzzi V7 V-twin and a Suzuki GT750 triple.

At the Monza race circuit the Honda performed very well, being the second fastest lapper, despite its high handlebars, putting in a best time of 2min 6.14sec against the Ducati's 2min 2.47sec. Third best on the track was the Laverda, almost six seconds in arrears. Given the reputation Italian makers had acquired for superior roadholding, this was a creditable performance for the Four.

Predictably, the Kawasaki two-stroke won on straight-line acceleration with a 12.17-second standing quarter-mile, but the Honda was third quickest after the Ducati with a 13.36-second run.

On top speed, the Honda was third again with 191km/h (118.69mph) behind the Guzzi's amazing 201km/h (125mph) and the Kawasaki's 194km/h

(120.5mph). The Suzuki was a trailing fourth at 179km/h (111.2mph). Motociclismo had obtained 194km/h (120.5mph) from the original CB750.

In weight rankings, the 222.5kg (490.6lb) K2 was third heaviest behind the hefty 231.5kg (510.5lb) Suzuki and the 223.5kg (492.8lb) Laverda. The lightest was the 189kg (417lb) Ducati.

The results confirmed the Honda's all-round ability.

Less accurate in its test methods, but interesting nevertheless, was a six-way comparison feature in the November 1970 issue of Two Wheels. Peter Chambers reviewed the half-dozen Superbikes available at the time in Australia: the BMW R75/5, BSA Rocket 3, Honda CB750, Kawasaki Mach III, Norton Commando and Triumph Trident. All were in standard trim, except for the Norton which had a tuned engine.

Machines were judged on key attributes and ranked in order from 1 (best) to 6 (worst) with the following result.

	Honda	BMW	BSA	Kawasaki	Norton	Triumph
Acceleration 0-50mph	3	6	=4	1	2	=4
Acceleration 50–100mph	4	6	5	2	1	3
Brakes	1	2	4	5	6	3
Low-speed handling	2	5	4	1	6	3
High-speed handling	4	5	3	6	1	2
Cornering clearance	1	2	6	3	=4	=4
Fuel consumption	2	1	3	5	6	4
Docility	3	1	5	6	2	4
Vibration	3	1	5	4	6	5
Comfort	2	3	1	4	6	5
Total:	25	32	40	37	40	37

On this table, where the lowest figure represents the highest ranking, the Honda rates best with an overall score of 25 against the BMW's 32, the Kawasaki and Triumph with 37 and the BSA tieing last with the Norton on 40. The CB750's scored best on braking and cornering clearance, and lowest on top-end acceleration and high speed handling.

These were Briar Brown (brown was a generally fashionable colour in the 1970s) Candy Gold, Planet Blue and Flake Sunrise Orange, but not all schemes were available on every market. The headlamp support brackets were now chromium plated and the lamp's shell finished in black, rather than matching the tank colour. A fuel filler cap change had already been implemented

during K1 production. The new cap needed two hands to release, which was considered safer than the thumb-latch type that could open accidentally in some circumstances.

The instrumentation was altered, most notably by siting the warning lights (popularly known as 'idiot lights' when they were still a novelty on motorcycles) in their own fascia built into a one-piece upper handlebar clamp. The speedometer and rev-counter now had metal, instead of plastic, outer casings.

The CB750's moderately changed appearance was accompanied by a more muted exhaust sound, thanks to the use of silencers with more efficient internals and smaller diameter outlets. Sadly, this spelled the end for the original Four's much loved racer-like snarl and helped to soften its general performance. All manufacturers were facing increasingly strict emission regulations being introduced by American legislation.

A revision of the rear suspension saw conventional Showa oil-damped struts replace the de Carbon type but their appearance was not greatly changed. The troublesome plastic rear chain guard was finally abandoned in favour of a pressed-steel type and on US machines the anti-jamming plate on the rear sprocket was increased in diameter, while the sprocket mountings were beefed up to overcome the known fault of them loosening in service.

The American-market K2 featured a revised rear lamp unit, which was enlarged and incorporated reflective panels on the side and rear surfaces of the lens for added night-time safety. With the high-performing 750 selling so well in the US, Honda was conscious of the need to be seen to take what safety measures it could to reduce the likelihood of accidents. Unlike many other manufacturers, Soichiro Honda met with the American consumer safety campaigner Ralph Nader early in 1971 and discussed motorcycle safety with him.

For similar reasons, US market K2 machines also introduced an audible warning device to remind riders to cancel the direction indicators. It consisted of a buzzer wired to sound repeatedly when the indicators were in use. Probably intentionally, the sound was irritating, but it could be muted by holding in a button set below the horn push on the left handlebar's switch cluster.

For added security, the seat now locked in its normal down position.

The next, K3 version, was released for 1973 on the North American market only while Honda continued supplying K2-coded machines in Europe, Australia and other smaller markets. These K2s incorporated various technical updates but remained cosmetically the same, always retaining the same seat cover, for example, where this feature changed annually in the USA. In the UK, the K2 continued to be sold until the end of 1975.

On the North American K3, the first major change of fuel tank livery saw the simple con-trasting stripe design replaced by black side panels edged with gold, white and black pin striping. The Honda badge remained, its white characters standing out from the black area. The main machine colours available were now a choice of green (Bacchus Olive), reddish-brown (Maxim Brown Metallic) or reddish-orange (Flake Sunrise Orange).

Complaints about the CB750's front suspension shortcomings were addressed on the K3, and the changes applied on K2s shipped elsewhere. The front fork had attracted particular criticism from US riders for the way it jarred over the regularly spaced expansion joints that are a feature of many US urban freeways. The problem was caused by sluggish reaction aggravated by point-loading at the bushes.

In response, an entirely new design of telescopic fork was adopted. Dispensing with the bushes, it used direct contact between the plated main tube and the internal surface of the aluminium lower slider as a bearing. The two-way hydraulic damping mechanism was also revised and rebound springs were added to prevent 'topping-out'. The fork sliders incorporated altered brake caliper mounting points, used with a changed bracket. Five pre-load settings were now available from the rear suspension units.

The US-only 1975 K5 retained the stripe-edged panel tank design. This example is in **Flake Apricot Red.** (John Colley)

From the K5, the cylinder head finning has a centrally placed pillar. (John Colley)

The K5's left-side fuel tap can be turned without using the throttle hand. (John Colley)

The speedometer dial is in 10mph increments from the K4 on. (John Colley)

The indicators on the K5 are common with Gold Wing fitments. (John Colley)

A mass of small alterations were motivated by safety considerations as well as the ongoing refinement of the machine following Honda's guiding principle of improving user-friendliness. These included enlarged rear-view mirrors and twin-filament bulbs for the front indicator lamps, which provided 'clearance lights'. Coming on with the headlamp, they were intended to increase the machine's visibility in day or night-time conditions. Handlebar switchgear was altered, transferring the headlight main and dip switch to the left side while the adjacent indicator control was modified so it could be pressed gently for short activation without the buzzer sounding, as well as being positively switched to bring the winkers on permanently.

Another safety device prevented the engine from being started accidentally when still in gear: the starter circuit remained dead unless the clutch lever was held in while pressing the button. The engine kill switch on the right switch cluster was moved to the site previously occupied by the dip switch, making it less prone to being inadvertently knocked to one of its two 'off' positions.

Easily checked wear markers were introduced on the front brake friction pads to stop owners wearing them down to the backing metal, and a small plastic guard was fixed to the rear of the left fork slider to stop rainwater being flung up on to the rider and the spark plugs by the disc rotor.

Round-profile passenger footrests were a K5 detail change. (John Colley)

A splash guard for the front disc was first introduced on the K3, for 1973. (John Colley)

The twistgrip on the K5 lacks a friction adjuster mechanism. (John Colley)

The relentless quest for silence, spurred on by impending US regulation, prompted a reduction in the size of the air-filter housing's intake aperture. The result was a reduction in intake roar, making the Four an exceptionally quiet motorcycle for its time, but a cut in engine performance was the inevitable side-effect. By now, the CB750 had to sell against the faster 900cc Kawasaki double overhead camshaft four that had usurped it as the ultimate motorcycle, as well as a liquid-cooled three-cylinder two-stroke 'Grand Tourer' from Suzuki. Honda's response seemed to be in accentuating the sophistication, civility and convenience of its 750, rather than trying to outdo rivals on raw performance.

K5 side panel badge lettering on a black background. (John Colley)

Growing opposition

In mid-1971, Kawasaki unveiled its 750cc H2, a bigger, wilder and thirstier version of its 500cc triple. But it was Kawasaki's double overhead camshaft 903cc Z1 Super Four which challenged the CB750's supremacy and shook the motorcycling world, in September 1972.

Yamaha, the second biggest motorcycle manufacturer after Honda, launched its first four-stroke for 1970. Targeted at Triumph twin fans in America, the 650cc XS1 (later XS650), had a solidly designed vertical twin-cylinder engine and sold steadily into the early 1980s. Yamaha's first 750, the TX750 eight-valve twin, flopped badly in 1974, but a 64bhp dohc triple with shaft drive fared better from 1976. The company's first roadster four was the gargantuan 95bhp XS1100 released in 1978.

Although Yamaha showed an exciting 750cc liquid-cooled, fuel-injected two-stroke four-cylinder roadster at Tokyo in 1971 and a radical 660cc rotary-engined machine in 1972, neither reached production. Exhaust emission controls steered all the major factories towards four-stroke engines. Yamaha changed course and by 1980 had set itself the ambitious target of deposing Honda as the number one motorcycle company.

Suzuki was still an exclusively two-stroke factory when it followed its first 'big' bike, a 500cc air-cooled twin, with the luxurious three-cylinder GT750 for 1972. But although two-strokes usually scored on lightness, the liquid-cooled Suzuki weighed in at 12kg (26lb) more than the CB750 and was clearly more the Grand Tourer its name suggested than a hot sportster.

Three years later, the bulky and unorthodox Suzuki RE5 Rotary, rated at 500cc, was in production, but not popular. With an eye to America's tightening emissions rules, Suzuki made its costly but successful switch to four-stroke power in 1976, principally with the GS750. A comfortable and reliable 68bhp dohc four weighing 223kg (492lb), it handled nicely and was capable of 123mph (198km/h). It immediately became the CB750's toughest 750cc market rival.

Britain's Norton remained a contender with its brisk, well-handling Commando, a capacity boost to 850cc being offered from 1974. The BSA marque collapsed, but production of an electric-start Triumph Trident staggered on until 1976.

Italy's Laverda gained a higher profile when its 1,000C triple appeared in 1976 and Ducati's new line of 750cc and 860cc V-twins were revered by sporting riders as instant classics. Moto Guzzi developed a range of 850 and 1,000cc sportsters and tourers featuring pleasantly lazy V-twin engines and rock solid handling that could eat up miles at high average speeds.

By the end of the Seventies, the Superbike focus had shifted up the cubic capacity scale and Honda pitted its dohc CB900 fours and CBX1000 six against an array of European and Japanese machines of similar or greater engine size.

Suzuki's GT750 triple rivalled the CB750 as a sports tourer (Author).

This K5 is now registered in the UK, where the reflective type of number plate became obligatory on new machines from 1973. (John Colley)

A lasting relationship

The moment that Pete Christian first saw the only CB750 present at the Isle of Man TT in 1969 he resolved to save up and buy one. Like other UK buyers, he had to wait until early in the following year to take delivery of his dream bike, bought from Ken Ives Motorcycles in Leicester, the nearest main Honda dealer to his home in Market Harborough, Leicestershire. Ives received machines from the first batch to arrive in the UK in January 1970.

'They said a blue-green bike was being delivered to the shop, but I was determined to have a red one, so they had it changed. It was the fifth CB750 they had sold,' explained Pete. Then a truck driver and seasoned motorcyclist in his late thirties, he traded in a 650cc Triumph Bonneville.

'My first impression after the Triumph was the Four's tremendous power and acceleration. Because of the high handlebars, there was terrific wind pressure on my chest at speed.' But after 5,000 euphoric miles Pete's bubble burst: the final drive chain snapped, resulting in badly damaged main engine cases.

'Strictly speaking, it should have been dealt with by the dealer, but I actually rebuilt the engine myself with a new set of crankcases given to me under warranty – on condition that I handed over the old ones.

'It didn't put me off, and over all the years since, the engine has hardly needed to be touched. It's still on the original air filter element.'

As often happens with the pre-1971 air-filter housing, it split and has been patched up with epoxy resin. After three years of ownership, more major repairs were forced on Pete by an accident.

'Two cars had a smash in front of me, I couldn't avoid them and went straight over the top.'

He cracked a bone in his neck – an injury only detected when he was X-rayed some years later – and the front end of the Honda had to be rebuilt, a job Pete did himself funded by the insurance pay-out. New parts used included fork stanchions and sliders, handlebars, a later pattern lipped front mudguard, a rev counter and a complete handlebar switch and lever assembly, as Honda could not supply a replacement for the snapped lever on its own. During the repairs, the headlamp bulb was uprated to a more powerful type.

One of the exhaust header pipes still bears a dent from that collision. Amazingly three of the silencers are original 1970 items but the upper left one,

Pete Christian with the bike he saved hard for in 1969 (John Colley).

The toolkit and seat filling are original - the plastic bag contains spare throttle cables (John Colley).

The main engine cases supplied under warranty did not have a serial number (John Colley).

normally the first to rot, had to be replaced and is the later K1 type but its outlet was modified to match the other three. The lower left silencer has been patched up where it corroded.

Pete is a high-mileage man, usually accompanied by his wife Rose. But UNR 887H has been well-preserved thanks to his owning and riding a series of other machines including two Honda CBX1000s and a six-cylinder Benelli. At the time of writing the CB750 had less than 40,000 miles recorded.

A Renold drive chain kit was fitted early in the machine's life, front fork gaiters have been replaced several times and a speedometer cable changed when it wore out. Throttles cables tend to break at the twistgrip so Pete always carries a spare.

An oil leak where the rev counter drive enters the cam cover was stemmed with a home repair and the petrol tap had body damage soldered by Pete and its internal seals replaced.

Some of the Candy Ruby Red paintwork has faded, but otherwise the finish has proved surprisingly durable with the exception of the rear mudguard's chrome plating which is starting to bubble up.

'It's an instant starter, better than my CBX. It rattles a bit and the carbs are well overdue for balancing, but it still cruises nicely on the motorway. The handling was never that good but I'm really glad now that I kept it.'

The combined 1975 CB750 and CB550 brochure for the US market. The accent was on relaxed two-up fun rather than aggressive sport riding.

Road Bikes   CB-750 K5 / CB-550 K1

'None of the refinements worked on the CB750 since its introduction seem to have been intended to make the bike any faster – and it is certain that none has had that effect,' observed *Cycle* in its test of the K3.

The secret of the Honda's success, it suggested, was the attention paid to improving the tiniest details which all contributed to an escalating level of reliability and user-friendliness. Points that still needed attending to were the rear brake, which *Cycle*'s man found too easy to lock up, and general standards of roadholding which could now be compared unfavourably with the smaller CB500 Four introduced in 1972.

By now the CB750 had become a familiar sight in every country where motorcycling was popular, appealing to riders of all types, from commuters and long-distance touring couples to

would-be racers who fitted dropped handlebars, loud aftermarket exhausts and even big-bore engine kits.

American motorcycle sales reached an all-time high in 1973, with more than 1.5 million units sold (excluding scooters). The CB750 was not entirely responsible for this since sales of smaller machines, especially dual-purpose trail bikes, were booming. Nevertheless, Honda had successfully addressed the growing demand for big, sophisticated bikes. The 1973 figure is rivalled by the highest-ever, 2002 US sales, forecast at the time of writing to exceed 1.6 million units, but that includes scooters and ATVs (all-terrain vehicles).

Developed to deliver the various recent refinements on the Japanese market CB750, the K4 also provided a 1974 update for the

Honda reversed a decision to phase out the basic CB750 to release the K6 for the 1976 season. Widely available on various markets, this version has the small indicators, long superseded in the USA. (John Colley)

USA. It exhibited mostly cosmetic revisions, consisting of a slightly altered tank panel design with a broader white stripe. On the speedometer dial, the scale was divided into increments of 10mph rather than 20mph as previously. Two fresh overall colours were added to the reddish-orange option, Boss Maroon Metallic (a plum red) or Freedom Green Metallic, while the olive green and brown schemes were dropped. Just to make the bike that bit more user-friendly, the gear change pattern was now cast into the transmission outer cover adjacent to the pedal.

From 1974 on, the external appearance of the cylinder head casting was noticeably changed. It now had three, rather than four, vertical bracing pillars visible on the side finning, one of them being placed centrally.

Despite a lean year for the North American automotive market in the wake of the 1973-74 energy crisis, the CB750 surprised pundits by being confirmed as the top-selling motorcycle in the USA at the end of 1974. Many had expected only smaller capacity machines to be in demand. In the following years, sales figures suffered from rising machine prices and insurance premiums, while the two-stroke roadster was to be banished from American roads on emission grounds.

Despite fluctuations, the market was becoming increasingly competitive for the CB750 as new large-capacity contenders kept coming from Germany and Italy as well as Japan. BMW now offered the 124mph (199km/h) R90S luxury tourer, Laverda added a 1,000cc triple to its range, and a change of management at Benelli had seen the launch of its spectacular six-cylinder 750 Sei.

The final K Fours of 1977 and '78 had revised styling, leaning strongly towards American tastes. This is the K7 – the North American market also had a K8 version with minor modifications. (John Colley)

The long run

British film maker Julian Grant demonstrated the CB750's ruggedness and dependability – and his own determination – when he rode one fitted with crash bars and luggage for 22,000 miles around the coast of Australia. Much of the journey was on rough going and Grant had several heavy spills on his K5, including one that forced him to repair his mount with parts from a fellow CB750 owner. He consumed two rear tyres, two drive chains and a few pep-pills in completing the journey in under 31 days. He had done it for a bet, but never collected the $20,000 wagered by American Frank Wheeler. Grant's exploits were featured in US Honda advertising material.

The K7's changed front indicator location and decorative 'Honda' plate. (John Colley)

Reshaped tank with a flush locking cover over the filler cap. (John Colley)

The rear indicators were moved back to join the tail light assembly. (John Colley)

The side-panel emblem, now with scrolled 'F' in 'Four'. (John Colley)

The biggest blow of all had been Kawasaki's release of its 903cc Z1 in 1973. With a claimed 82bhp and a top speed in the region of 130mph (209km/h), the dohc in-line four represented the biggest superbike milestone since the CB750's appearance. Although it had some handling deficiencies, the mighty and durable Kawasaki instantly took over as the ultimate volume-produced speed machine, forcing Honda to market the CB750 more on the strength of its reputation for general usefulness and dependability, rather than sheer performance.

In 1975, Honda's headline-grabber was the 1,000cc GL1000 Gold Wing. With a liquid-cooled flat-four engine, shaft drive and luxurious specification, the new 130mph heavyweight usurped the CB750's position at the top of the company's range. In the USA, two CB750 options were made available for that year. The established model continued in K5 guise, while the new-look CB750 F Super Sport promised a livelier alternative (see next chapter).

The latest K machine incorporated various minor improvements, several being safety related. To help prevent mishaps caused by side-stands not being retracted before a rider set off, a device that would be seen on various Hondas was added. Simply a rubber tail on the stand leg, it was designed to brush the road before the main leg grounded, and flip the stand up out of harm's way.

The K5's direction indicator lamps were enlarged by adopting the Gold Wing type. Re-positioning of the fuel tap from the right to the left side was also a positive safety measure, since the rider no longer had to release the throttle or front brake when reaching down to switch over to reserve. Minor changes included a different throttle drum which no longer offered friction adjustment of the twistgrip action. The only colour options for 1975 US Ks were Flake Apricot Red or Planet Blue Metallic.

Motorcycle press reviews were beginning to suggest that the long-running CB750 was becoming too bland and lacking in character.

'It's an awfully good motorcycle, perhaps too good to be exciting,' *Cycle Guide* concluded in its mostly positive K5 test, saying the Four had become a victim of its own success and popularity, thereby losing the ability to be exotic. This fickle aspect of the motorcycle market has always provided headaches for Honda and has helped the sale of rival machines from smaller makes, even if their reliability was not as certain.

Yet the K's following proved to be stronger than even Honda imagined. A cool reception for the Super Sport variant was accompanied by protests at Honda's admission that it planned to phase out the basic CB750. Bowing to pressure, the company reprieved the K model and a sixth update featured in the 1976 range.

Superseding the K5 in America, the K6 was also available in the other markets around the world which had not seen a significant update since the K2. All the K3 to K5 updates were incorporated, with the exception of the enlarged indicators, which were not adopted across the board. Machines delivered in Germany had a slightly reduced power output of 63PS (62bhp). In the UK, the indicator warning buzzer had not been introduced because of concern that it constituted a hazard at lights-controlled pedestrian crossings, where blind people might confuse the sound with the bleeper that indicates when it is safe to cross.

New K6 features included the Super Sport's strengthened swinging arm and revised mounting for the instruments, which now had green dial faces. A plastic under-seat tool tray replaced the sheet metal type which was prone to splitting, apparently as a result of frame flexure. The carburettor idling adjustment screw was resited more accessibly on the right of the machine, while internal carburettor settings were revised and further softening of engine performance made the K6 slower than its predecessors.

In the transmission, the clutch was made a tighter fit on its shaft and secured by a circlip. The oil distribution system at the final drive chain's front sprocket was phased out.

Testing the K6 for the US magazine *Motorcyclist*, former racer Jody Nicholas concluded that the K's evolution to date had improved its handling and reduced the characteristic transmission snatch. He approved of the Dunlop K81 Gold Seal tyres and generous seat filling on his test bike. Gripes included a noisy clutch, clunky gearchange and poor relative positioning of the indicator and horn controls. Overall the K6 was rated as excellent value for its purchase price and described as: 'one of the most respected and sought-after touring machines this country has ever seen.'

By 1976, Honda had sold 100,000 CB750 Fours when a third variant was launched on the North American market for that year in the form of the novel CB750A with semi-automatic transmission. Honda offered the Hondamatic model in the hope of enticing new male and female customers on to motorcycles, particularly in the new climate of concern over the amount of fuel consumed by a typical American automobile. The CB750A Hondamatics are described in the next chapter.

For 1977, Honda came up with fresh versions of all three CB750 variants. The touring all-rounder came in the guise of the K7, which was markedly changed from the K6 and had acquired many F-type features. These included a power unit with similar specifications to that of the 1976 F1's with a 9.2:1 compression ratio, sports camshaft and more closely spaced gear ratios. The 28mm Keihin PD carburettors had enclosed throttle-lifters and one of them was now fitted with a diaphragm-type accelerator pump mechanism, also present on the latest F2 version of the Super Sport. Linked by tubing to the other three instruments, this delivered a jet

of neat petrol into each venturi as the throttles opened. The system countered hesitancy in pick-up which resulted from the weakening of the mixture needed to reduce emissions in line with America's Environmental Protection Agency regulations.

Along with the 1977 CB750 F and CB750A models, the K7 benefited from a final drive chain with lubricant-retaining O-ring seals. Used with sprockets of revised design to suit it, the 630-size chain was endless, having no split link.

The revised styling veered towards an American custom type, with no gaiters on the front fork. A deep fuel tank with its filler concealed under a hinged flap was shared with the automatic model, but on the K it carried a gold stripe edged with red and white pin striping. The overall colour choices were Candy Alpha Red or Excel Black.

A new style of side panel appeared and the upper silencers' heat shields were now absent from the four-pipe exhaust system, being considered unnecessary as the passenger footrests had been resited to positions above both silencers. The effect was to make the silencers look neater, especially as they no longer had raised seams running along their length.

Conventional spoked wheels were retained but with wider steel rims and a 17in rear rim was now fitted which wore a wider, 4.50-section tyre. In the USA, it had been fashionable to fit older Fours with smaller, 17in or 16in wheels. In theory, the fatter tyre provides enhanced touring comfort. The single-disc front brake was kept and in most cases so was the rear drum, an exception being the rear disc-equipped K7 for the Japanese market. This odd model also had the alloy footrest hanger plates as seen on its F2 Super Sport contemporary and had a slightly lowered power output of 65bhp, because it lacked the F2-type camshaft.

Following F-model practice, the rear suspension units now had wholly exposed springs without shrouds, but on the K7 the coils remained plated. Travel was increased by 25mm over the K6 units. The indicator lamps were common with the GL1000. Their front mounting stalks were now set at the same level as the lower fork yoke and both these and the headlamp brackets were chromed. There was an extra embellishment for the upper fork assembly in the form of a front cover for the lower yoke, which carried a Honda badge. There were now two horns, mounted side by side ahead of the frame downtubes with high and low tones that combined to give a sharp warning note.

Australia's *Two Wheels* said that the K7 was not the best 750 on the market, but believed it still had a lot to offer the budget-conscious rider who wanted to cover high mileages with ease. The tester liked the engine but noted warming-up was a long process and that mechanical noise was excessive. The sohc unit was noticeably noisier than rivals' newer dohc engines. The suspension was praised, along with rider comfort and the stability of a chassis that was 25mm longer than the K6s, but criticisms were made of the braking and the K7's general bulkiness. In

the UK, *Motorcyclist Illustrated* called the K7 mild but meaty, pointing out that while the CB750 was now outclassed on performance and handling, it could still appeal to riders seeking dependability and comfort above all.

Towards the end of 1978, Honda's long-awaited double overhead camshaft in-line fours reached the showrooms. Two 750s, the CB750 KZ and the CB750 FZ sport version were joined in Europe by a 900cc CB900 FZ and in the USA only a custom-style limited edition of the 750 with special trim was released to commemorate the 10th anniversary of the 750 Fours.

Like factory endurance racers campaigned in Europe since 1976, the new engines featured four valves per cylinder as well as twin camshafts. There were many similarities between these units and the one powering Honda's latest Superbike sensation, the 135mph (217.25km/h) six-cylinder CBX1000, also introduced during 1978. In the meantime, updated versions of the K (now the K8, logically enough), the F and the automatic had been listed for the 1978 selling season on the North American market.

Minor cosmetic changes apparent on the K8 included a two-tier seat with the passenger portion set slightly above the rider's and yet another side panel emblem, now accompanied by a painted stripe. Technical alterations included minor changes in the top end of the engine, even leaner carburettor settings and a front brake light switch activated by the handlebar lever rather than the hydraulics.

Stocks of the F2 and K7 remained to be cleared from European showrooms, the official discontinuation date for these models in the UK being May 1979, although the F2 was still listed in the UK-published 1980 edition of the *World Motorcycle Guide*.

Offshoots of the original

Super Sports

When Honda introduced the GL1000 Gold Wing for 1975, the CB750 lost its position as the company's flagship motorcycle. To give the 750 four a new lease of life and fend off new challengers from other makers, Honda launched a derivative with a more sporting image, initially on the American market. The CB750 F Super Sport was still powered by the familiar in-line four-cylinder, five-speed power unit, but there were many significant internal changes and the machine as a whole was remodelled.

Like the CB400F Super Sport launched in 1974, the 750cc Super Sport was cosmetically influenced by 'cafe racer' style. On the F this included a four-into-one exhaust system, an elongated fuel tank and a seat-tail moulding incorporating a roomy tool locker.

Honda UK had played a part in the Super Sport makeover as Gerald Davison, a senior manager of the wholly owned subsidiary at the time, recalled: 'In Japan, the best R&D people were preoccupied with the car side of the business which was at make or break – it had to succeed or it could have brought the whole company down. We came up with ideas for a new sports machine that could be implemented at the factory without the need to go through the R&D stage. We put forward chassis improvements and proposed more flowing lines – what we called the Euro Sport look.'

Although it had the same quoted 67bhp as the K-series fours the Super Sport engine, now numbered with an F suffix, it delivered its power in a noticeably revvier way, thanks to extended cam timings and higher valve lift, compression ratio upped slightly to 9.2:1, and gearing alterations.

The primary drive's reduction was increased to 1.985:1 and the final drive ratio lowered by the use of a smaller, 17-tooth output sprocket while inside the gearbox the fourth and fifth ratios were altered. The net result was closer spacing of the ratios and a lowering of the overall gearing, by 23 per cent in the lower three gears and by 27 per cent in the top two. Engine revs were consequently higher at any given road speed but the exhaust noise was more subdued than ever thanks to a large, rather ungainly, single silencer.

To match the higher engine speed, the red sector indicating maximum rpm on the rev-counter dial began at 8,500rpm. That had actually been the 'redline' on the earliest Ks before being edged down to 8,000rpm from the K2 onward, but on the F it was now deemed permissible to occasionally hit 9,500rpm.

Launched on the US market in 1975, the Super Sport had leaner looks and lower gearing. Having all four exhaust pipes swept to the right leaves the left side looking incomplete. (Honda)

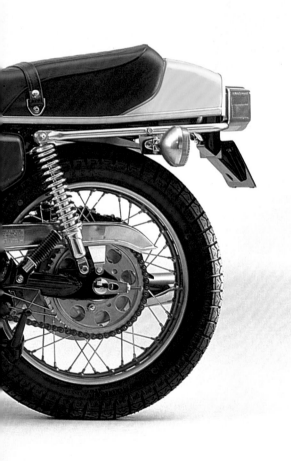

Frame alterations created increased front fork trail, which was accompanied by a lengthened wheelbase, and accommodated the F's more rearward set footrest assemblies and brief rear mudguard. Suspension movement was increased in both the fork and the rear suspension units, where both compression and rebound damping had been uprated. Rear wheel braking was now by a disc, on the right side of the machine with the caliper mounted above the axle and linked to the unsprung portion of the frame by a torque arm. Useful improvements over the basic CB750 included a tougher specification for the final drive chain, beefing-up of the swinging arm and a headlamp that was brighter despite being smaller in diameter.

Less praiseworthy was the dropping of protective gaiters for the front fork in the interest of meaner looks, an oil filler now only accessible when the right-side panel was removed and one single seat hinge replacing the two provided on the Ks. The seat now lifted from the right, which made sense in right-side driving markets. A moulded carrier box, which also formed the upper part of the rear mudguard, provided handy stowage space under the seat's tailpiece, but had an annoying ability to trap water.

The restyled fuel tank increased fuel capacity to 18 litres (4gall) and had a lockable filler lid to prevent accidental spillage and the consequent fire hazard. It also made the top of the tank smooth, removing a projection that was a potential cause of horrific injury to the rider in a collision. To prevent it being left behind at filling stations, the cap under the lid was attached to the tank's interior by a chain. Dry weight of the CB750 F was quoted at 223kg (490lb), showing an increase over the K5's 218kg (480lb).

Cycle World liked the Super Sport's handling, describing it as 'better than any other standard

Seeley: handling, style and exclusivity

Between 1975 and 1978, the English company Colin Seeley International was responsible for 309 neatly crafted Seeley Hondas with CB750 engines and other running gear. The majority of the Seeleys were supplied as chassis kits to which engines were added, but a number were commissioned as complete motorcycles, using brand new Hondas as donor machines.

Former sidecar GP racer Colin Seeley had founded his own marque in the 1960s to build road racers around single-cylinder ohc 350cc AJS and 500cc Matchless engines, to which he had acquired manufacturing rights.

After the British singles became outpaced by Japanese two-strokes, Seeley decided to embark on a CB750-based project in the winter of 1974-75. He purchased a new K2 and set about reworking it with the aim of creating a top-quality road-legal motorcycle that was lighter, better handling, better looking and easier to work on than a standard CB750.

A tailor-made frame was designed, to be made by Seeley's welder Jack Wren, in the same light-gauge Reynolds 531 tubing as the Seeley racers. Of duplex cradle layout, it was well braced at the steering head which contained taper roller bearings and was set at 28°. The swingarm featured the simple and precise chain tensioning system devised for Seeley racers and substantial sheet-metal gusseting supported its pivots.

The earliest of the series retained many original Honda components including the instruments, front fork, brakes, exhaust system and even the seat. However, Seeley subsequently produced racer-style single and dual seats to match his handsome 20 and 25-litre aluminium tanks and used various proprietary parts. Kits were added to convert F1 and F2 models as well as the K series.

Cast alloy wheels were sourced from Campbray in the UK and later from the US company Lester, when Seeley became its UK agent. Other American

Class act: a 750cc Seeley Honda with nickel plated finish on its Reynolds 531 frame. The exhaust system is Seeley's own four-into-two. (Colin Seeley)

A 1000cc Seeley with special edition white-enamelled frame and black cylinder block. (Colin Seeley)

components used on some machines were Hunt plasma-coated aluminium brake discs, Jardine exhaust systems and S&W rear suspension units. Seeley also devised his own four-into-two exhaust system and his frames were usually finished with nickel plate, although an F2-powered limited edition sported an unusual but eye-catching white enamel frame.

Some of the Seeley Hondas sold as complete bikes had US-sourced big-bore kits giving capacities of 810 and 1,000cc.

Although some UK dealers, including Read Titan, were distributors for the costly Seeley Honda, most examples were exported to a total of 12 countries. For the German market, where a significant number of kits and machines were sold, the necessary TUV approval was obtained. Seeley also negotiated imports to Spain, despite that country's embargo on fully Japanese motorcycles.

Like Seeley's racing machines, the re-framed Hondas were noted for superlative roadholding, elegance and exclusivity.

large Japanese bike'. Improved stability at speed and when passing trucks in a cross-wind, plus better flickability on twisty roads were remarked on as gains over the basic CB750 in *Cycle Guide*'s test.

But, on the whole, the Super Sport failed to elicit anything like the excitement that had greeted the original CB750. This, of course, was partly thanks to the general raising of customer expectations that came in the wake of that outstanding launch. And possibly, to the heightened skills of road testers who had been sampling a succession of high-performance superbikes for several years.

While *Cycle Guide* liked the brisker acceleration brought about by the engine and transmission changes, its tester complained of poor throttle response at the bottom-end of the rpm range, worse vibration than on the K models, and increased fuel consumption. The F averaged 38mpg (US) against *Cycle Guide*'s figure of 42.6mpg for the K5, at a time when the price and conservation of fuel were topical subjects.

Notchy gear changes, transmission whine and intake roar were all noted, but *Cycle Guide*'s tester pointed out that these may merely have become more noticeable thanks to the increased

muffling of exhaust noise. Despite the introduction of a rear disc, the magazine's braking distance figures for the F were inferior to those of the K5. This was explained by the need for caution in order to avoid locking the rear wheel under heavy application of the new-style disc brake.

The tester complained of a deterioration in handling after 700 miles, apparently caused by a fall-off in damping from the rear shock absorbers. *Cycle World* noted un-Honda-like compromise in the Super Sport's build quality and finish, pointing to the single-hinged seat that waggled when raised and the cheapskate look of the black tank-top lid and side panels. One of its testers admitted to disconnecting the indicator buzzer, removing the seat-top strap and changing the handlebar grips before taking a prolonged tour through California's Gold Rush country.

In speed tests, *Cycle Guide* achieved better acceleration than from the K5 with a standing quarter mile at 13.10 seconds, but concluded that top speed was pretty much the same at a shade under 120mph (193km/h). He must have ridden a very good K5!

The CB750 F Super Sport's sales were sluggish in America and feedback from potential

On the F, a chain secures the fuel filler cap under its lockable lid. (John Colley)

The red zone on the rev-counter now extends to 9,600rpm. (John Colley)

The F1's rear disc brake, with its caliper anchored by a torque arm. (John Colley)

The lifting seat reveals a luggage box under its tail section. (John Colley)

The Sulfur Yellow scheme put many off the first Super Sport. (John Colley)

customers suggested that many preferred the classic Honda Four with its four prominent megaphone-style silencers. This bore out what Bob Hansen had told Honda back in 1968, that four pipes were essential for image, if not for performance. It should be mentioned, though, that many CB750 owners around the world were fitting aftermarket four-into-one exhaust systems with derestricted silencers which were enjoying popularity as a performance booster, whether real or imagined.

The 'Euro' styling didn't seem to be appreciated in the USA either, but for 1976 the Super Sport continued in the form of the barely altered CB750 F1 and was now listed for the Australian and European markets as well. A similar model was sold in Japan as the CB750 F-II. The original Super Sport is now inevitably referred to as the F0.

The colour choice for the F1 changed from 1975's Candy Sapphire Blue or Flake Sunrise Orange to 1976's Candy Antares Red or Sulfur Yellow, the latter being a lurid colour of the type usually seen on cafe racers or other customs rather than production machines.

Several UK press testers questioned the Super Sport label. Usually applied to uncompromising high-performance semi-racers, it was seen as something of a misnomer on what was really a sensible, comfortable and versatile machine. *Bike* magazine pitched the 1976 F1 against the Suzuki GT750A, the new pepped-up version of the water-cooled triple. Its conclusion was that the Suzuki was sportier than its bulky tourer looks suggested, while the Honda was the best all-rounder of the two, despite a misleading model name.

Praising the Honda for its dry-weather handling and high-speed stability, *Bike* thought the F1 showed some consideration by Honda for riders other than the 'American Mr Average cruising at 55mph'. Points of criticism included a fuel range of barely more than 100 miles (161km/h) and tyres and brakes that performed poorly in the English rain. Delayed action from wet disc brakes was becoming a major issue at the time.

John Nutting of *Motor Cycle* was more impressed, since his test figures proved the F1 to be considerably faster than the K, mainly thanks to higher rpm in top: the basic CB750s had a fifth gear that acted like an overdrive. He reported reaching 106mph (170km/h) normally seated and completed a run at 122.34mph (196.85km/h) in a racing crouch.

Demonstrating that for all the criticism levelled at it, the CB750 F1 was still an extremely useful

motorcycle, a trio of Australians touring Europe bought second-hand examples in England and rode them home. Their route took them overland through Yugoslavia, Turkey, Iran, Afghanistan, Pakistan and India. Then a sea crossing was made to Singapore where the bikes were put on a ship for Perth while their riders flew ahead. Ironically, it was on their last home leg of the journey from Perth to Sydney that the group suffered their first flat tyre and ran out of fuel for the only time on the whole adventure.

The Hondas were given routine servicing en route and performed reliably, despite having to run on poor, 82 octane fuel at times. The only component failure reported in an account of the trip published in *Two Wheels* was a damping oil leak from one rear shock absorber.

Super Sport F2

The really marked performance boost that was lacking in the Super Sport finally arrived for its third season. Making a postponed debut in North America at the beginning of 1977 and released some months later elsewhere, the CB750 F2 had its power output usefully boosted to a claimed 70bhp and a top speed of 125mph (200km/h) in favourable conditions. Just as importantly, it had a fresh look as well.

The F2 Super Sport gave Honda some ammunition with which to defend itself against the recent dramatic arrival of Suzuki's GS750. Having decided it must adopt four-stroke power for most of its roadster range, Suzuki made sure of getting its double overhead camshaft in-line four-cylinder engine right from the start, by closely following Kawasaki's successful pattern.

Enthusiastically received, the GS750 combined sizzling 125mph performance with easy European-type handling and set new standards for sports 750s.

The Super Sport F1, as imported to the UK in 1975–76. The four-into-one exhaust system feeds into a large single silencer. (John Colley)

The revamped Super Sport for 1977. The F2 had a tuned engine, altered silencer, twin-disc front brakes and Comstar composite wheels with steel spokes riveted to alloy rims. (John Colley)

Brake calipers are placed behind slimmed front fork sliders.
(John Colley)

To achieve engine performance in the same league as the twin-cam Suzuki, Honda engineers used classic tuning techniques on the existing engine. In the F2's reshaped combustion chambers, the inlet valve heads were of 34mm diameter against 32mm on the previous roadster 750 engines, and up from 28 to 31mm on the exhaust side. Performance was also enhanced by fitting Keihin PD carburettors with an accelerator pump and fully enclosed throttle mechanisms, as on the K7. The red zone on the F2's rev counter started at 9,500rpm to suit the higher tune of the engine.

Areas of plain metal relieve the F2 engine's mainly black finish. (John Colley)

Aftermarket goodies

Once the CB750 had become established on the market a variety of kits, from bolt-on makeovers to complete frame replacements, appeared in several countries.

London Honda dealer Read Titan of Leytonstone had a makeover kit on the market in the autumn of 1970. Comprising a large capacity aluminium fuel tank, racing seat and clip-on handlebars, it followed the cafe racer fashion that had been popular in Britain for several years.

Paul Dunstall had been in the tuning and customising business for several years when the CB750 arrived. By 1971, his South London company listed a 'Dunstallised' CB750 along with his famous modified Norton twins. Among the performance parts offered were 10.25:1 high-compression pistons and paired two-into-one systems devised for Dunstall by racing, exhaust specialist Dr Gordon Blair of Queen's University, Belfast. Altered cycle parts included Girling rear units, Italian Borrani aluminium wheel rims and Dunlop TT100 tyres. The tank and seat were in moulded glassfibre, although a regulation introduced in the UK during 1973 would ban plastic tanks on newly registered vehicles, forcing customising companies to sell only aluminium items. With a large, 19-tooth gearbox output sprocket, Dunstall's 750 hit 127mph (204km/h) on test with *Motor Cycle News* in 1972.

The subsequent Dunstall Devastator had a capacity of 889cc, a gas-flowed cylinder head and special camshaft. Producing 80bhp at the rear wheel, the Devastator clocked a rather disappointing 122mph (196km/h) when tested by *Motorcycle Mechanics* in 1976.

As its CR750 model designation confirmed, the Rickman Honda announced in 1974 was also in the cafe racer mould. A complete package rather than a cosmetic kit, the Rickman housed the CB750 power unit in a largely British-made rolling chassis. Founded by motocross racers Derek and Don Rickman, the company originally made lightweight frames and bodywork for off-road sport. By 1966, road race chassis to suit AJS and Matchless single-cylinder engines were added to the repertoire and roadster derivatives followed, to accept Royal Enfield engines and Triumph units in both twin and triple form.

The CR conversion of a donor CB750 could be carried out in a working day by a skilled person. The kit was based on a typical Rickman frame of double-cradle design, made in large-diameter Reynolds 531 tubing. The swingarm was controlled by Girling units, while front suspension was by Rickman's own two-way damped fork with stout main tubes. The steering head angle was 29°.

Track-style equipment included a long fuel tank with knee recesses, a seat with a rear stop, clip-on handlebars and rearset footrests. The exhausts, oil tank and side panels were among stock Honda parts retained and a fairing was optional.

Rickman cafe racers on display, with a complete CR750 on the right and an assembled kit minus donor Honda parts in the centre. The machine on the left is a Kawasaki-powered CR900. (Derek Rickman)

Frenchman Gilles Langlois and his unusual Zerchot-framed special at the 1999 Montlhéry Coupe Legende Festival, where a special display marked the 30th anniversary of the CB750. The French Zerchot concern made a small number of racing frames for the CB750 in the mid-1970s. (Author)

big-bore 950SS transformation based on the standard frame appeared in 1972 followed two years later by the 1000 VX in basic, Vitesse and Bol d'Or variants, the latter having the enormous fairing used by Japauto endurance racers from 1973. Their 970cc engines had a special, 70mm-bore cylinder block casting identifiable by its coarse finning. Combined tank and seat mouldings and four-into-one systems with collector boxes were among other Japauto products. An estimated 1,000 kits were sold and 150 complete machines exported to Spain.

After building a frame for his own CB750, Georges Martin went into business making them for others. His Moto Martin company, originally in Paris and later at Sable d'Olonne on the Atlantic coast, produced wheels and bodywork as well as frames for the CB750 and a wide variety of other engines. The Moto Martin powered by a six-cylinder CBX1000 engine is probably the definitive model of the type.

In the USA, Yoshimura R&D produced a complete modified CB750 Daytona Special in small numbers and countless other companies listed individual tuning and customising parts. They included Action Four and Powroll for big-bore kits, and Bassani, Kerker, and Hooker for exhausts. Probably the best known apart from Yoshimura was RC Engineering, supplier of big-bore kits, Golden Rod con-rods, camshafts and other tuning aids as well as exhaust systems. RC's proprietor, Russ Collins, gained fame across the world by drag racing an awesome 12-cylinder machine powered by three CB750 engines linked by rubber belts. Nicknamed the Atchison, Topeka and Sante Fe, after the famous railroad company, it was unreliable and handled atrociously but nevertheless took Collins to the world's first sub-eight seconds (7.86sec) quarter mile at Ontario raceway, California in 1975 with a terminal speed of 179mph (283km/h). After a near-fatal crash, Collins bounced back with a supercharged twin-CB750 engined eight-cylinder dragster which made a 7.55-second run, reaching 199.55mph (321.08km/h).

Praised for rock-steady handling and strong braking from twin 250mm Lockheed discs, the Rickman version weighed around 20kg (44lb) less than a stock CB750. However, its virtues of high-quality construction were accompanied by annoying vices such as fiddly drive chain adjustment at the swingarm pivot, and the absence of a fuel reserve.

Rickman CRs were exported around the world and the CB750 kit was joined by a variant to accept 900 and 1,000cc Kawasaki engines as well as post-1977 Honda dohc fours.

In France, the Parisian dealer Japauto marketed various kit parts, initially sourcing from Read Titan. A

Russ Collins with *The Sorcerer*, the supercharged and fuel-injected twin CB750-engined 2,000cc dragster built for 1977. It reached a whisker less than 200mph on the standing quarter mile. (Mick Woollett)

There are one main and four small outlets in the tapered silencer's end cap. (John Colley)

The indicators are by the rear light on UK F2, but further forward on the US type. (John Colley)

The ignition switch and choke are adjacent to the instrument cluster. (John Colley)

The throttle-lifters are enclosed on the 28mm Keihin PD carburettors. (John Colley)

A number of internal engine changes, including uprated bearings for the crankshaft assembly and stouter cylinder studs, were made to cope with the boosted output. Externally, the most noticeable difference on the F2's power unit was its satin black finish, relieved by retaining chrome-plated contact breaker and clutch housing covers and plain metal for the alternator casing's outer face.

The black engine finish (not seen on Japanese-market models which also had higher handlebars) had helped reinforce the super sporting image, since it was usual to finish road racing engines in that colour to improve their heat-radiating properties.

In Europe, marketing linked the F2 closely with Honda's devastating endurance racing campaign launched in 1976. For the French catalogue, an F2 was photographed on the Le Mans circuit, the venue for the hugely popular Bol d'Or 24-hour marathon. The company could claim with some justification to have race-developed the CB750, but in reality, the 170mph (274km/h) RCB fours with which it stormed the European endurance series were markedly different, having engines with dohc and four-valves-per-cylinder top ends in special chassis.

The roadster's frame geometry was tweaked further by a steeper head angle and the wheelbase was now quite lengthy at 1,500mm (59in) but the Super Sport F2's most noticeable chassis feature was its novel Comstar wheel, developed in the rigours of endurance racing.

A radical departure from the traditional motorcycle wheel with wire spokes in tension, the Comstar composite item made for Honda by DID, had a rolled-aluminium rim and a cast-aluminium hub. They were linked by five spokes formed by bringing together left and right star-shaped steel pressings, bolted to the hub and fastened to the rim by rivets.

One-piece cast aluminium and magnesium-alloy wheels had been seen in road racing since the early 1970s. They were introduced on BMW roadsters in 1976, but disastrous crack failures delayed their widespread adoption and the German company paid the price of innovation.

New dohc engines arrived in 750 and 900cc form from 1978. This is the sporting CB900FZ. (Honda)

The Comstar design was claimed to offer the best features of both wire-spoked and cast wheels, combining strength with a degree of flexure and minimum unsprung weight. Its drawbacks were that it was more difficult for owners to keep clean than the cast type and could not be re-trued after a minor accident as a spoked wheel often could. Also, many people thought the new wheel looked rather odd, and even ugly.

Honda pioneered the use of tubeless motorcycle tyres on Comstars in its 1978 range, but would eventually drop composites in the 1980s, when cast types had been perfected.

Twin-disc front brakes were now generally perceived as a necessity for any large capacity bike with sporting pretensions. On the F2 they took the form of 275mm rotors and Nissin single-piston calipers carried on horseshoe-shaped castings bolted to the fork sliders. They followed a trend of the time in being sited behind rather than ahead of the fork legs, where they were said to be less likely to have a bad effect on steering inertia. The rear wheel was braked by a single 250mm disc and a caliper that matched the front type.

The F2's exhaust system was easier on the eye than the earlier four-into-one, now having a tapered silencer with a pronounced upward tilt and a matt black end-cap of more than 125mm in diameter.

Although the tank, seat and side-panel bodywork were otherwise essentially the same items as on the earlier Fs, new paint schemes gave the machine a fresh look. The base colours were a black, Candy Presto Red and a Candy Sword Blue base colour with a gold and white-edged contrasting flash of reddish-orange on the tank sides. Where the earlier Super Sport's side panels were black, the F2's matched the tank and seat moulding base colour.

Suspension travel had been increased both in the front fork and the rear units. The gaiterless front fork now had slimmed lower sliders with vertical frontal ribs, finished in satin black. Internally, damping was further improved and springing was lighter. The chromed headlamp support brackets and similarly finished indicator stems were of similar style to those on the 1977 CB750 K7.

A new pattern of Showa rear shock, the FVQ shared with several other Hondas in the 1977 range, provided two-stage damping. Not externally adjustable, the internals were designed to give a light response when riding over minor undulations yet automatically stiffen up when harder shocks were delivered. The progressively wound dual-rate springs were adjustable for pre-load. Neat cast-alloy footrest hanger plates carried both the rider's and passenger's footrests on each side. A gutter placed just below the seat on the right side of the frame was meant to run rain water clear of the rear disc.

Testing the CB750 F2 in August 1977, *Motor Cycle*'s John Nutting made a timed one-way run at over 128mph, benefiting from a tail wind. The two-way mean came out at 124.6mph and 108mph with the rider seated normally. But the standing quarter-mile time of 13.5 seconds was a shade slower than *Motor Cycle* had managed with the F1. The difference was ascribed to extra weight offsetting the power boost and less flexibility across the rpm range. Handling was said to be improved again over the F1 and practical points on which the F2 scored highly were strong braking, a bright headlamp, effectively loud twin-tone horns and its O-ring drive chain. As in some other F2 tests, the tuned engine's moderate thirst for fuel, returning an average of 45mpg (UK), drew favourable comment.

Two Wheels suggested with Australian frankness that the F2 might be seen as merely 'an old whore with a face lift' but said that in fact, Honda had 'given the old girl a hormone injection, making the engine feel new and different.' The latest four was described as 'refined, comfortable and at the same time it has reserves of excitement that many government bodies are trying to kill.'

The tester asserted that the F2 was 'probably the best-braked Japanese bike yet' and that as on the GS750, riding at under 6,000rpm was easy and at over 6,000rpm, quick. Low speed behaviour was praised, except for the oft-quoted 'falling-in' to slow corners. *Two Wheels* panned the 'hopeless' headlamp but rather liked the loud horns.

A minimally changed F3 incorporating minor engine changes continued on the North American market for 1978. It was externally identifiable by changed '750 Four' lettering on its side-panel emblems.

As the ultimate incarnation of the CB750 before Honda's long-awaited double overhead camshaft replacement appeared, the F2 was viewed as a mere stop-gap to temporarily fend off strong opponents such as the 750cc dohc Suzuki and Kawasaki's nippy and pretty dohc Z650 four. As a result, it probably did not the receive the full credit F2 fans believe it deserved for its happy blend of strong performance and typical CB750 practicality.

Putting on the style

The coming of the CB750 coincided with, and contributed to, a sea change in Britain's motorcycling scene.

Japanese products moved on to high ground that ailing home factories could no longer defend. An often predictable and inward-looking motorcycling press was shaken up by the brighter, less reverential approach of *Bike* magazine, launched in 1972. Also, riders were abandoning traditional black leather or waxed cotton in favour of brightly coloured riding gear and the latest helmets with full visors meant they could make long journeys, even in bad weather, without covering their faces with road grime.

Seeing a new marketing opportunity, Honda UK announced its Honda Style collection of modern clothing and bike accessories in 1975. The range of apparel included UK-made leather suits, jackets and jeans, waterproof oversuits and helmets, some sourced in the UK and others from Italy. Fairings, luggage racks, crashbars and other hardware was produced by other UK manufacturers, principally Rickman.

Honda Style clothing had a common theme based on dark green with striping in white, mustard yellow and a lighter green. Gerald Davison, the Honda UK boss behind the concept admitted that more design work was executed in his kitchen than by fashion consultants.

Either because the colours didn't appeal, or because motorcyclists found the whole idea too conformist, Honda Style clothing did not catch on in a big way. Surplus stocks were disposed of in other European markets.

A more significant development of the time, also master-minded by Davison, was the Honda Five Star dealer scheme intended to raise standards of service for customers and encourage loyal Honda dealers to develop. He explained: 'The idea was to bring the trade up to date, with diagnostic equipment, better training and clinical workshop conditions.'

Other promotions of the mid-1970s included the introduction of Honda-branded lubricants and appearances by the glamorous Miss Honda, beauty queen Dinah May.

Just too corporate? The Honda Style brochure depicts Honda people inhabiting a super-bland world.

Automatic for the people?

Honda has always prided itself on being an innovatory manufacturer. Some of the company's most adventurous ideas have met with tremendous success while others have failed to spark great enthusiasm from the buying public. The 750cc Hondamatic represented a fascinating technical exercise in producing a version of the CB750 Four with semi-automatic two-speed transmission, but it can't really be said to have succeeded in its intended role.

The idea was to encourage members of the American public who would not otherwise consider buying a large capacity motorcycle to enjoy the freedom, practicality and economy of two-wheeling. Since automatic transmissions were in almost universal use on four-wheeled vehicles in the USA, it was believed that reducing the frequency of gear shifting could make a motorcycle less intimidating for riders seeking an economic commuter machine in the post-energy crisis climate. With its proven record of usability and reliability, the CB750 was seen as the best model to adapt in creating the first Hondamatic.

Honda was not the first make to offer a semi-automatic transmission mechanism on a motorcycle: earlier types had been seen on British BSA and Zenith products and the Czechoslovakian Jawa. A successful system based on a hydraulic torque converter was developed in Italy by Moto Guzzi, whose 1,000cc Convert semi-automatic shaft driven V-twin had been launched for 1975.

Although it was displayed at the 1975 Paris Show and several examples reached Europe, the 1976 CB750A was only marketed in Japan and North America, where it was priced at a few dollars more than the F1 Super Sport.

Visibly, the Hondamatic was a close relative of the established 'manual' Fours. The forward part of its power unit was similar to the other models' with their familiar inclined cylinders and crankcase, but obviously the rearward part containing the transmission was much altered, especially on the right side, where prominent alloy and plated-steel covers enclosed an oil-filled torque converter mechanism.

Overall, the 1976 automatic was easily distinguished from its K and F contemporaries mainly thanks to a higher capacity fuel tank and a deep luxury seat with a built-in passenger grab rail at its rear. The side panels were of a new shape to match the seat and they carried the Hondamatic legend.

The wheels were built with DID aluminium alloy rims shared with the GL1000 super tourer and as on that model, the rear wheel was of only 17-inch diameter and wore a 4.50-section tyre.

Other parts common with the Gold Wing included the front mudguard blade, while the disc front brake was shared with the CB750F and the exhaust system was similar to that model's in having a four-into-one configuration. Colour options were Candy Antares Red and Muscat Green Metallic, the scheme looking rather stark without tank striping.

A normal foot-operated gear lever was provided on the right of the power unit, but in this case it selected only three positions. It was eased upwards to change from neutral to low and then up again for drive, while pressing it down to the lowest position returned it to neutral. An indicator showing the Neutral, L and D positions was displayed in the right-side instrument binnacle used for the rev counter on the other Fours, along with a set of warning

The parking brake knob with release button under the left side of the tank. (John Colley)

A linkage under the selector pedal connects the side stand to the transmission. (John Colley)

The left side of the power unit is little changed from the 'manual' CB750. (John Colley)

The large round housing contains a fluid flywheel mechanism. (John Colley)

lights, indicator repeaters and a simple needle-type fuel gauge.

To set off in low, the rider simply snicked up the pedal and could then travel to a maximum marked on the speedometer dial at 60mph (97km/h) before engaging drive which then gave step-less acceleration up to the claimed 105mph (169km/h) maximum. For more leisurely riding, it was also possible to use drive to set off from a standstill.

Devoid of a handlebar clutch lever, the CB750A had a number of necessary added features. Like an automatic car, it had a park brake mode. Pulling a knob under the left side of the fuel tank outwards while pressing the brake pedal locked the rear drum brake on by means of a cable linkage. To release the brake, the rider depressed the foot pedal while pressing a button in the centre of the under-tank control knob. Other safety measures were a cut-out to prevent the starter operating unless the transmission was in

The side panel moulding is shaped to follow the line of the deep seat. (John Colley)

neutral, and a mechanical rod linkage on the side stand which automatically engaged neutral when it was lowered. An emergency kick-start lever was supplied detached, stored under the seat.

The workings of the transmission were based on a semi-automatic two-speed system Honda had developed for car use some years earlier. The main engine oil supply was used in the elaborate hydraulic system which meant that there was sufficient overall capacity to dispense with the frame-mounted tank. Doubled-up oil pumps were installed in the lower main casing, one to supply the engine and the second to maintain pressure in the transmission's hydraulics, which could reach more than double the engine's normal oil pressure. The plumbing was designed to avoid excessive heat build-up.

The primary drive's conventional roller chains were replaced by a more resilient but heavier Morse Hy-Vo inverted-tooth chain. It was of a similar type to that on the CB500 Four. The change necessitated using a new crankshaft assembly with the requisite teeth cut into its centre portion. Drive was taken to a jackshaft from where reduction gears propelled the torque converter, which used an oil-filled turbine system to transmit motion and multiply torque from the engine to the gearbox mainshaft.

The change mechanism consisted of a three-way hydraulic valve operated by the foot pedal and a pair of hydraulically operated multiplate clutches – one for the low gear pinions and one for drive – located on the gearbox shafts and activated from the valve. Engaging one of the clutches by shifting the pedal would route the power through the applicable gears and to the output shaft.

De-tuning of the Hondamatic's engine was accomplished by fitting lower compression (8.6:1) pistons with a milder camshaft and reduction of the carburettor choke size to 24mm. To ensure good pulling from low revs, an accelerator pump system similar to that on the K7 and F2 was included. Power output was a modest 47bhp at 7,500rpm.

In its test of the CB750A, in which it compared the Hondamatic with the 1976 F1, *Cycle World* decided that the power disadvantage would be unlikely to trouble riders spending much of their time in heavy traffic and reported that the automatic was a pleasure to ride on the Los Angeles freeways in the rush hour traffic. Seat comfort on the A model was applauded and the generous cornering clearance noted, although to achieve it the footrests were set higher, causing discomfort for taller riders. The suspension was criticised for being harsher and stiffer than on the F-type. Braking distances were found to be similar on both machines while tested maximum speeds were recorded as 110mph (177km/h) from the F1 and 97mph (156km/h) from the Hondamatic.

On the whole, *Cycle World* concluded that sporting riders wanting to explore mountain roads would much prefer the sharper performance of the Super Sport. Some doubt was also cast on the idea that the automatic would draw new people into motorcycling. It was suggested that novices would prefer something lighter and less bulky.

One of the few CB750As that reached Europe was evaluated by John McDermott of the UK magazine *Motorcyclist Illustrated* in its September 1976 issue, which incorporated a 16-page supplement promoting Honda Style products and Honda lubricants. McDermott collected the Candy Antares Red Hondamatic while at the June Isle of Man TT and began his 2,000-mile test by reeling off two laps of the Mountain Course, liking the effortless way it cruised along straights and through fast sweepers. Finding foot changes between low and drive jerky, he opted to stay in the higher ratio, but as a result found more braking was necessary than with a 'manual' bike when shedding speed in twisty sections where its bulk made it less than nimble. Admitting to feeling slightly out of control at times at first, once familiar with the automatic McDermott found it easy to trickle through heavy traffic. He marked it down on long-range comfort and described drive

Hard luggage was available for the 1977 Automatic, which has a four-into-two exhaust system and stepped seat. (Honda)

chain stretch as 'horrific'. His conclusion was that the CB750A was not for the scratcher, but rather for the rider seeking a machine suitable for both daily commuting and long-distance touring.

The 750 Hondamatic remained in production for three seasons and revisions for the 1977 CB750A1 improved its appearance. The exhaust system was now of four-into-two configuration, terminating in an upswept tapered silencer on each side. This facilitated fitting of luggage panniers available as official accessories. The dual seat was now a two-tier type, like that which would appear on the following year's K version, and the integral grab rail disappeared. Colour schemes were now Candy Presto Red or Candy Sword Blue and restrained gold pin striping was applied to the tank and side panels. In Japan it carried the enigmatic EARA model name. The final CB750A2 of 1978 acquired Comstar wheels and was offered in Candy Alpha Red or Candy Polaris Blue.

Fewer than 9,000 CB750A automatics are believed to have been sold, a figure that Honda must have found disappointing, especially in view of the complex design and engineering involved. The company, which also marketed a Hondamatic CB400AT version of its 395cc twin-cylinder commuter from 1978 to 1981, learned that most motorcyclists found operating a foot-change transmission more satisfying than having semi-automatic drive. In the case of the CB750A, its excessive bulk (262kg/577lb dry in 1977 form) and not particularly frugal fuel consumption opposed its worthy aims of being utilitarian and rider-friendly.

In recent years, alternative forms of automatic transmission have enjoyed a revival on two-wheelers, being a feature of 'twist-and-go' scooters of all sizes.

The roadster that raced

For a machine designed as a grand tourer, the CB750 enjoyed remarkable success on the race track. It is thought that the first of the Fours to contest a road race was an absolutely stock machine entered for a meeting at Harewood, Ontario during May 1969. Ridden by Canadian Mike Manley in a race for production machines, the Honda led for the first two laps but eventually had to settle for third place behind former Yamaha works rider Mike Duff on a Norton Commando and Roger Beaumont on a Triumph Trident. Being ridden hard straight out of the crate without special setting-up, the Four lost out to its rivals on handling.

More important for Honda was publicity gained from victory in the 10-hour endurance race for production machines run in August at Japan's Suzuka circuit, which was originally built as a Honda facility in the early 1960s. Coinciding with the CB750's launch in the country, the event was won by the two-man team of Sumiya and Hishiki, with Oguma and Sato second on another Four. The riders were all members of Team Blue Helmet, Honda's staff racing club.

Winning another prestigious event, France's historic Bol d'Or (Golden Bowl) endurance race, gave the Four an excellent European promotional boost in September 1969 just when the initial waves caused by its launch earlier in the year were beginning to settle.

The 'Bol' had been established as a 24-hour marathon for production machines in the 1920s but dropped off the calendar after 1960. Renewed interest in motorcycling throughout France saw it revived in 1969, as an arena in which the speed and reliability of new models could be tested publicly.

The venue was the atmospheric Montlhéry track on the southern outskirts of Paris, which features spectacular 'speed bowl' bankings, often used in the past for speed record attempts. Honda, who had not fielded official machines in a road race for two years, shipped two specially prepared CB750s to Alf Briggs at Honda UK to be entered in the 'Bol' by Bill Smith Motors.

The plan was for them to be ridden by Smith, Tommy Robb (a former Honda GP teamster), rising star John Williams and Smith's employee, Steve Murray. In endurance races, teams of two or more riders take alternative stints of several hours in the saddle.

Special parts fitted in Japan included hotter camshafts and a special exhaust system. No air filters were fitted and power output was up to 72bhp. The machines also sported clip-on handlebars, a long slim aluminium fuel tank, single seats and fairings.

The team was supervised by Yoshio Nakamura, a leading light of Honda's Formula One car racing team. But when it arrived at Montlhéry the organising club said that there had been a misunderstanding. This was not an international

Michel Rougerie en route to Honda's first Bol d'Or victory in 1969. Then 19 and unknown, Rougerie went on to be a prominent GP rider. (Alain Rouge)

A Daytona track marshal holding a fire hose looks at the crumpled and burnt remains of Ralph Bryans's crashed Honda during practice for the big race. (Mick Woollett)

race and it was only open to French riders. All attempts to get round the problem failed and so Nakamura agreed to lend one of the factory bikes to the Parisian dealership Japauto, replacing one of the near-stock CB750s it had entered. The machine would be shared by 19-year-old French students, Michel Rougerie and Daniel Urdich.

Japauto, unfamiliar with a racing CB750, requested technical help in their pit and Steve Murray obliged. Prior to the race he took a clip-on from the spare bike and clamped it to a fork tube below the bottom yoke to carry a car spot light, augmenting the headlamp for night riding.

The relatively inexperienced riders measured up to their task by winning. Not without incident, though, for during the night the Honda's engine cut and its lights went out. Rougerie pushed to the pits where a faulty headlamp switch was by-

passed by Murray and the blown fuse replaced by silver foil.

Two Laverda entries had presented a serious threat to Honda, one setting the fastest lap time, but both of the Italian parallel twins dropped out before the end of the race. A few hours from the finish a 500cc Kawasaki two-stroke triple was leading, but then it had to come in for a drive chain replacement. The Honda, which had its chain lubricated during pit stops sailed on and took the flag first.

Averaging 72mph (116km/h) for the 24 hours, the Four completed 445 laps, a distance of 1,742 miles (2,803km). A second near-standard CB750 entered by the importer finished fifth, completing 401 laps. Rougerie went on to be one of France's top racers, winning three GP races, but lost his life in a crash in Yugoslavia in 1981.

Dick Mann on Daytona Speedway's twisty infield section during his winning ride in the American 200-mile race in 1970. (Mick Woollett)

The Bol d'Or success did wonders for the Honda CB750's public image in Europe, especially in the French and German markets where it was exploited in advertising. But in the wider world it was victory in America's prestigious Daytona 200 event in March 1970 that proved the Four's potential.

Bill Smith had a major role in this enterprise, too, but the true heroes of the Daytona story were Californian-based veteran racer Dick Mann and Bob Hansen, American Honda's national parts manager. Hansen's background was in racing and in 1967 he orchestrated Honda's first entry in the springtime 200-miler with CB450 racers. Although the racing twins showed promise, the factory dropped them in 1968 to concentrate on CB750 development.

When the 450s contested the 200-miler

(322km) the rules restricted overhead valve engines to 500cc, but allowed side-valve engines of 750cc, as fielded by Harley-Davidson. This archaic formula was to be dropped for 1970, when 750cc engines were allowed across the board. But the traditional insistence that machines be based on production models was maintained.

Not surprisingly, Hansen canvassed Honda Japan to enter the CB750 at Daytona: 'At one of our meetings I suggested we entered 750s at Daytona. The initial response was that it would be better not to, in case we lost. I turned the argument around and pointed out that of our 1,200 dealers in the States some would be bound to enter Hondas at Daytona, and they wouldn't be likely to win. So it would be best if we made a really first-class official effort.

The full kit

Although the racing version of the CB750 is almost universally referred to as the CR750, this is not a designation given to it by the Honda factory. The company produced a range of CR racing models from 50 to 305cc in the 1960s, but they were complete machines supplied via dealers and road-legal versions were released on the Japanese home market.

The CB750 Racer, as Honda prefers to call it, took different forms. A very small number, including the official Daytona entries, were assembled to race-ready form in Japan incorporating special lightweight components.

Other CB750 Racers were produced using some or all of the components from the kit of parts supplied by RSC (Racing Service Centre), the specialist department at Honda which preceded today's HRC (Honda Racing Corp). The Four created from this kit is sometimes referred to as the Senior.

Comprising at least 180 parts, from major components to sundries such as washers and O-rings, the entire kit was almost prohibitively expensive, and very few were issued. The large capacity aluminium fuel tank alone was more than half the cost of a complete CB750 roadster. Consequently fully kitted machines were rare.

A third category of CB750 Racer is sometimes referred to as the CYB750, as it was roughly equivalent to CYB350 and CYB250 roadster-based racers sent to Europe. These 750s had the ordinary kit specification, but were built by RSC in Japan and shipped complete. A pair of this type were supplied to UK Honda dealer and racer Bill Smith in 1972.

The race kit was still available in 1974, when an American Honda bulletin listed the components and part number under the heading 'Honda CR750 Racing Parts', a rare use of the CR term in official documentation.

Power from a fully kitted CB750 Racer was claimed to be 90bhp at 9,500rpm. On high gearing, the top speed was in the region of 150mph (240km/h). Dry weight was 175kg (386lb) and aerodynamic efficiency was vastly improved over the stock machine.

The following were the key constituents of the CB750 Racer kit:

Engine
Inlet valve 32mm and 33.5mm
Exhaust valve 26mm and 27mm (larger than standard)
Valve springs (special material)

Cylinder head (greater fin area, altered porting)
Forged 10.5:1 pistons and rings (higher compression)

Camshaft (higher lift, longer duration)

Set of four Keihin CR 'smoothbore' carburettors with 31mm venturis

Spark plug caps

Cam chain, guides and tensioner (lighter and stronger)

Cam cover with bosses for eight extra camshaft securing studs

High-strength steel connecting rods

Primary chains

Oil-cooling radiator

Small, CL350-type twin-pole ignition generator (reduces engine width)

Close-ratio gears

Exhaust system (originally four pipes with reverse-cone megaphones, later four-into-one)

Cycle parts
Replacement front fork with twin disc front brake, including fork sliders with four-stud wheel spindle clamps

Replacement swingarm, with clevis mounts for suspension units

Rear brake hub and backplate assembly for twin-leading-shoe operation

Alloy front wheel rim and complete rear wheel

Rearset footrest assemblies

Brake and gearchange linkage foot controls

Rear suspension units

Aluminium fuel tank and fuel tap
Aluminium oil tank

Clip-on handlebars
Front fork top yokes
Instrument bracket
Small rev-counter
Fairing and brackets

Several frame alterations were required to convert a standard chassis to racer specification, mainly involving added or altered bracketry. A fairing and tachometer support bracket was added to the front of the steering head and lugs added to support the centrally mounted oil tank. A solid mount for the left footpeg replaced the tubular passenger footrest mount on the left side and frames were modified to carry a gearchange linkage to suit the resited footrests. Some machines had right-side gear changes to suit riders who were used to the old-style layout.

Full factory CB750 Racers had complete special frames made in superior material and modified at the steering head to alter geometry and improve ground clearance. Some had various magnesium alloy parts including engine casings, front fork sliders and fuel filler caps.

A batch of five factory-pattern frames were built in Britain during the latter part of 1972 by chassis specialist Spondon Engineering in Derbyshire. These were commissioned for European endurance racing by Honda France, who provided the drawings.

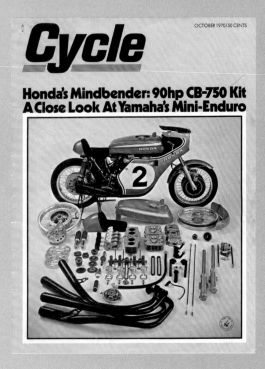

Headlined as Honda's Mindbender, the entire CB750 race kit was shown along with a complete kitted bike on the front cover of Cycle in October 1970. The feature inside warned readers that the special parts were virtually unobtainable.
(*Cycle*)

'Harada asked me how fast the bikes would need to be and what the lap times were. I picked numbers that were better than anyone had actually gone. He called me back after a few days and said: "we'll be there". He said they had fed horsepower and frontal area figures through a computer, and the top speed I quoted could be achieved.'

Hansen had envisaged two machines at most, but the factory built a quartet of CB750 racers, all conforming to a copy of the American Motorcyclist Association technical rules he had sent to Japan.

Originally, machines were to be assigned to riders entered by Honda UK: Robb, former Honda GP rider Ralph Bryans, Smith and

Murray. At Daytona, the team would again be supervised by Nakamura.

At a late stage, Honda decided it would be politic to have at least one American, and asked Hansen to recruit one. He contacted Dick Mann, America's Grand National champion in 1963. Recently with BSA, Mann had not been offered a ride with the British marque's team, being seen as past his prime at 36. He attended an interview at American Honda and struck a deal.

Four CB750 Racers arrived in the USA from the factory, numbered 101, 102, 103 and 105 because, rather ironically in the case of the Honda engine, the number 4 is considered unlucky in Japan. Hansen recalled: 'I think they figured Bryans would win and gave him 101.

Dick Mann with the winner's trophy and *Miss Motorcycle Classics 1970* in Daytona's victory circle. Triumph-mounted Gene Romero (No. 3) was second and Don Castro (BSA) third. (Mick Woollett)

The Dresda dimension

Dresda Autos of south-west London achieved fame when proprietor Dave Degens won the 1965 Barcelona 24-hour race on his own-built Triumph-Norton hybrid, partnered by Ian Goddard.

The pair won the race again in 1970 on a Dresda Triumph twin, with a double-cradle frame of Degens's own design and manufacture. As a result, he was approached by Christian Vilaseca of Japauto with a view to building chassis for his team's endurance racers. Degens was flown to Paris and lent an empty CB750 engine around which a purpose-built racing frame could be made.

'It was the first Honda Four engine I'd seen, because they were still a rarity in Britain then,' recalled Degens, who had the satisfaction of seeing one of his Japauto chassis win the 1972 Bol D'Or, followed by two more among the top six finishers.

On his Japauto Fours, Degens found that the four-into-one exhaust system he designed for extra cornering clearance had the desirable side-effect of improving torque out of corners and he became convinced that a wide, heavy engine, plus weighty double-disc brakes and the fuel load demanded a fairly long wheelbase for sound handling. Ingeniously, he routed oil to the cooling radiator through a portion of the frame tubing, gaining extra capacity.

A derivative of the Japauto chassis was supplied for the semi-official Honda UK machines raced on UK short circuits in 1976.

Dresda's business included building road specials for customers and with the demise of the British industry Honda engines began to replace the Triumph twins and triples in its workshops.

Whole batches of Honda-powered Dresdas styled like endurance racers were shipped to Spain. They were for an importer who circumvented the ban then in force on Japanese motorcycle imports. For this reason, they incorporated as high a proportion of Dresda, rather than Honda, parts as possible. As well as Dresda frames made in the usual Accles & Pollock T45 tubing, they had magnesium alloy cast wheels by John Cernhan, REH forks, Dresda

footrests and engine outer covers, plus UK-made fairings. Honda rear hub assemblies were machined and shrunk into rear wheel castings.

Twin front lamps were fitted to the Japauto bikes to help riders maintain speed at night for 24-hour racing and they became a trademark of Dresda fairings. A pair of Cibie units was used, one being permanently dipped and the other a high-beam lamp which could be switched on when needed. Degens recalled a visit from the UK transport ministry to warn him that his style of twin headlamps should not be fitted to road motorcycles, in case other road users confused them with cars. By the mid-1980s numerous makers were selling roadsters with twin headlamps, albeit set closer together.

Dresda Hondas displayed at shows usually sported gaudy Seventies' paint applied by the Leon Wallace specialist customising business a few doors along the street from Dresda Autos in Putney. Degens admits that the schemes were 'a bit silly' and recalled that the grossest example adorned a competition prize given away by the UK weekly *Motor Cycle News*.

A Dresda-framed CB750. Later versions had cast wheels, twin-disc front brakes and bolder paint schemes.
(Dresda Autos)

Tommy Robb with one of the four factory machines in the
Honda team workshop during Daytona practice. (Steve Murray)

Mann, whose US racing number was 2, got 102. The bikes all varied slightly, some being more special than others. I was surprised at some of the exotic stuff on them, such as titanium and magnesium.'

Used mainly to shed weight, these special metals were impractical for use on normal production machines, titanium being extremely expensive and magnesium alloy castings being highly inflammable as well being prone to rapid corrosion.

Steve Murray, who travelled with the British party as mechanic and reserve rider, said that titanium fork bottom yokes had to be removed in the USA under factory orders as they were thought likely to crack. He also recalled changing crankcases, as the magnesium items distorted when cooling down, locking up the engine.

The Daytona Speedway was built in 1959 primarily for stock car racing round a super-fast banked tri-oval, but for the 200-mile motorcycle race it comprised (as it still does today) a twisty, flat infield section as well as the banked sections. In 1969, it lacked a chicane that exists today on the approach to the northern bankings, so the racers' engines were held flat-out for even longer periods.

In practice, Bryans unofficially clocked 164mph (264km/h) on the bankings, indicating that the Hondas were up to speed. But then, running-in a new set of tyres, the Scots rider crashed after turning the power on too suddenly as he ran on to the banking. His bike burst into flames – quite spectacularly thanks to the presence of magnesium – and was too badly damaged to be rebuilt for the race, forcing Smith to pass his bike to Bryans.

Some tensions arose between Hansen and the British crew during the build-up to the race, and as a result, Hansen told Nakamura that he would only take responsibility for the performance of Mann's machine.

Top Pop

Yoshimura was probably the best known of the companies supplying high-performance equipment to suit the CB750. It was founded by Hideo Yoshimura, who had tuned motorcycles and cars since 1954 in his native Japan. Not confining himself to locally made products he worked on BSA and Triumph machines owned by US servicemen.

'Pop', as he became known, set up the American arm of his business in Southern California in 1971. Yoshimura R&D offered tuning parts for Honda's popular CB350 and the growing numbers seeking to hot up CB750s for road or track use. Sourced from several suppliers, Yoshimura products for the CB750 included a range of camshafts, 812cc big-bore kits, oil coolers and four-into-one exhaust systems.

Although once employed by Honda to restore old GP machinery, which he measured and logged meticulously in the process, Yoshimura was entirely independent. Indeed, when his racing engines outshone official entries, he was not exactly Honda's favourite person.

Numerous tuners claim to have been the first to fit a four-into-one exhaust to the CB750, but Pop developed his version on Honda S800 car engines before transferring what he'd learned to the motorcycle unit. In the mid-1970s, Yoshimura marketed the Daytona Special, a complete 750cc Honda-powered roadster.

Dixon Racing, run by former pressman David Dixon, took on distribution of Yoshimura products in Europe and South Africa at the end of 1972. Dixon became an admirer and personal friend of Pop.

'He treated engines as a complete package rather than going for piecemeal power boosts. He always liked to leave a safety margin. For example, he never took the CB750 engine out beyond 812cc, because he believed that removing cylinder block metal and inserting new liners to go higher would reduce cooling efficiency and jeopardise reliability.'

Pop Yoshimura died in 1993, but the company carried on under Hideo's son Fujio and is still a force in US road racing and the aftermarket parts field.

In the late 1970s, Honda and Yoshimura had close ties within the UK, since Dixon Racing was also a Honda dealer. Among many CB750 engines passing through Dixon's Surrey workshops was that of an F2 press machine which had its top-end blueprinted with the aim of turning in the best-possible standing-quarter-mile test times.

YOSHIMURA

Hideo Yoshimura in 1980. (David Dixon)

When the oil in Mann's engine was being changed, particles of rubber and metal were spotted in the drained fluid, indicating that the camshaft drive chain tensioner was breaking up. Seeing that this weakness could cost Honda the race, Hansen had Mann start the race with a brand-new chain and tensioner.

Held in spring sunshine on Sunday, March 15, the race was a serious battle for prestige in the US market. Ranged against the Hondas was a team of six triples, three in BSA colours and three Triumphs, specially built for the event and ridden by US and UK riders. The Triumph ridden by Californian Gene Romero had been the fastest pre-race qualifier, lapping at 157.34mph (253.16km/h) on the banked tri-oval used for the purpose.

Despite their capacity disadvantage 500cc Suzuki and 350cc Yamaha two-strokes were also in contention, although they needed to make more fuel stops than the four-strokes. Harley-Davidson's brand-new overhead valve XR750 was less of a threat, suffering engine problems related to overheating.

When the 200-mile epic got under way, Mann took an instant lead, but was then led by the British triples of former GP World Champion Mike Hailwood on a BSA and Triumph's Gary Nixon, who both led before their engines failed. The CB750s of Bryans and Robb dropped out, too, when their camshaft drives broke up. Suzuki's dark horse, Ron Grant, moved to the front on his 500 twin before he, also retired.

This left Mann out ahead, being pursued by Romero who had fallen and remounted on the first lap. Despite its new cam chain, in the latter stages of the race the Four began to go 'off song', causing some consternation in the Honda camp, but Hansen remained cool: 'I gave Dick a pit signal on each lap, telling him his position. He was slowing with cam chain trouble, but I had worked out that if he lost a second a lap he could still win. It was all under control, but when I was out on the trackside grass with the signal board, Mr Nakamura jumped over the pit wall and came running over to me, saying I had to tell Dick to go faster. But I had my "race face" on and just told him to get right back behind the wall.'

Mann used all his finesse to nurse the ailing machine over the finish line, 10 seconds ahead of Romero's Triumph, having averaged a speed of 102.69mph (165.23km/h) for almost two hours. He had opted for very high overall gearing, despite the concerns of Japanese technicians that it would prevent him reaching the engine's optimum rev range.

Satisfied with the Daytona victory, Honda did not sustain a full US racing campaign. Hansen recalls that by the time he returned to Honda's West Coast HQ new management was in place and he received a cool reception despite his record of success.

American homologation rules required that special parts used to convert standard models for racing had to be available commercially. Honda conformed by listing an extensive range of components with which non-factory teams and privateers could convert roadsters to race trim.

Yoshimura, a Japanese tuning company which had just set up a branch in California, was a principal source for the special parts as well as developing its own specialities such as racing camshafts and big-bore kits.

In 1971, 20-year-old rising US star Gary Fisher sensationally led the first four laps of the Daytona 200 on a Yoshimura-tuned Honda Four entered by Pennsylvania Honda dealer and Dunlop tyres distributor Ronnie Krause. Unfortunately, Fisher's race ended when his cam chain failed after only 11 laps.

The team returned to Florida in 1972, when Fisher had a convincingly lead after 35 laps but had to pull out when oil from a split tank reached the rear tyre. A second Krause machine, ridden by former Harley-Davidson teamster and Daytona 200 winner Roger Reiman, suffered clutch problems.

Racing parts for the CB750 were available for several years, but by the mid-1970s both Yamaha's 105bhp TZ750 pure racing two-stroke four and Kawasaki's 900cc Z1 roadster had elbowed the Honda out of both Formula 750 and the newly popular Superbike class in the USA.

Even so, a second official Honda attempt on the Daytona 200 was made in 1973 with a three-bike team managed by Nakamura. The riders were Reiman, Steve McLaughlin who later found fame on Superbikes and Morio Sumiya, a development rider for Honda RSC (Racing Service Centre). Sumiya had been in the

Morio Sumiya's factory CB750 Racer, now in Honda's
museum at the Motegi race circuit. (Honda)

victorious Blue Helmets team at Suzuki in 1969, won three Japanese championships on fours and had raced a Daytona-type CB750 racer at Britain's Mallory Park in 1970.

The 1973 version that Sumiya had played a major role in developing featured various refinements such as a four-into-one exhaust system and a slimmer fairing. It also carried Honda's new red, white and blue race livery.

But the reign of bellowing four-strokes in Formula 750 racing had ended and 350cc Yamaha two-stroke twins took the top three places, headed by Finnish 250cc GP champion Jarno Saarinen. Sumiya was the most successful Honda rider, finishing in sixth place, two places behind the top four-stroke finisher Dick Mann, aboard his BSA triple. Sadly Sumiya, one of the most talented racers to come out of Japan, was killed testing prior to the 1975 Bol d'Or.

Island debut

Winning the 750cc Production race at the Isle of Man TT meeting would have completed a remarkable hat-trick of wins in prestigious races for Honda in 1970. After Daytona, a UK weekly whetted fans' appetites by reporting that three of the factory machines would be at the June event, suitably modified to meet Production rules, such as full silencing and standard carburettors.

In the event, a trio of comparatively standard CB750s were specially prepared under the supervision of Alf Briggs at Honda UK and entered under dealers' names. The Production TT was run under a national licence, unlike the international GP class races.

Two of the official Fours started in the race, ridden by Tommy Robb and leading UK short circuit ace John Cooper, but they did not handle

well on the island's bumpy 37.733-mile (60.712km) Mountain course. Robb, who was also slowed by an oil leak, finished in eighth place ahead of Cooper in ninth.

A speed trap on a slightly downhill section of the course clocked Cooper at 136.9mph (220.3km/h), making his the second fastest machine in the race behind Paul Smart's Triumph Trident. Robb recalled that lack of power was not a problem, while poor roadholding was: 'The steering was pretty diabolical. I only weighed 9 stone (57.15kg) and I felt like a rat being shaken by a terrier. When I caught up with John [Cooper] I could see how his bike was wiggling and twitching as well.'

The race was dominated by factory BSA and Triumph triples, but in hindsight, Alf Briggs considered that his charges had done reasonably well in view of how standard they were. He continued to enter Fours for races, including the 1974 1,000cc Production TT, in which Charlie Williams finished fifth and was the fastest speed trap machine in the race at 133mph (214km/h).

Bill Smith, who maintained close links with Honda, obtained a pair of works-assembled CB750 Racers in 1972, just in time for John Williams and himself to compete in Italy's inaugural Imola 200 run to a Daytona-type formula. They were not among the front runners, finishing seventh and 12th respectively, but they and others rode them in subsequent TTs.

Italian CB750-mounted riders at Imola that year included Roberto Gallina, Silvio Grassetti and Luigi Anelli. The latter had the distinction of racing the original machine of the now-famous Bimota marque, built around a CB750 engine, and raced in 1973.

Prince of privateers

UK rider Peter Darvill, seen here racing in the 1973 Barcelona 24 Hours at Montjuich Park, had a successful career as a privateer entrant on Hondas in European endurance racing. His original racing Four was one of the very first machines to arrive in Britain in 1970, bought from dealer Bill Smith and converted for use on the track with open exhausts, clip-on handlebars and a fairing.

'That particular bike was very quick and reliable,' recalled Darvill, who finished second with French co-rider Olivier Chevallier in the 1970 Bol d'Or behind a factory Triumph triple and ahead of many other CB750s. Teamed with Norman Price, the gritty Brit was third at Barcelona in that year, a result he repeated paired with Ron Baylie in 1972.

The machine was constantly modified and for 1973 Darvill was able to obtain a better-handling works frame off the jig at Spondon Engineering which was used to make a batch for Honda France in the previous year. He obtained a second from the same source in 1975.

Seconded to the official Honda France team on several occasions, Darvill also raced CB750s in the Production and Formula 750 Isle of Man TTs in 1970 and '71. His career was unfortunately ended by injuries resulting from an accident in the 1976 Barcelona race, when his machine was rammed by another rider.

(Photograph courtesy of Mick Wollett)

Enduring passion

During the 1970s, endurance racing enjoyed a phenomenal upsurge in France and several other European nations, reflected by crowds exceeding 150,000 attending the most prominent events such as the Bol d'Or, which moved to the Le Mans Bugatti circuit in 1971. An expanding round of events included other 24-hour races over Belgium's ultra fast Spa-Francorchamps course and the Spanish Barcelona spectacular run on twisting public roads in the hillside Montjuich Park. Shorter events included races at Rouen in France and at Mettet in Belgium. From the mid-1970s, when an FIM Coupe D'Endurance Championship was inaugurated, a round was held at Thruxton, England, although endurance never generated the same fervour in the UK as it did elsewhere in Europe.

Always facing strong opposition, the CB750 was a mainstay of endurance grids through the 1970s. Official entries were made by Honda France and Honda Suisse (Switzerland), which was set up in 1974, while a variety of Fours in standard and special chassis were fielded by

Britain's race replicas

Honda UK marketed two batches of special edition race replicas based on the 1978 CB750 F2. The first was known as the Phil Read Replica and commemorated Read's victory in the 1977 Isle of Man TT Formula 1 race. The Honda Britain Replica was issued after a dispute arose between Read and Honda UK over royalty arrangements.

Following the TT win, Honda UK's publicity-conscious Eric Sulley contacted Colin Seeley International with a view to making machines to exploit the success. Seeley's expertise was widely known and Honda UK had looked favourably on the Seeley Hondas produced since 1975.

Under his contract, Seeley was supplied with CB750 F2s on which to carry out cosmetic modifications. They included changing the fuel tank, seat, exhaust system, modifying the handlebars and controls, then fitting a race-style fairing with twin headlamps. Machines were finished in Honda Britain's red, white and blue race team livery and the earlier version carried the words Phil Read Replica in script on either side of the fairing. Engines were left in standard F2 trim.

A total of 150 Phil Read Replicas were built, followed by 250 Honda Britain machines assembled at Seeley's new factory at Erith, in Kent.

Colin Seeley with a Phil Read Replica in Honda Britain colours. Its silencer copies the TT Formula 1 racer's.
(Colin Seeley)

Tommy Robb racing a Honda UK-prepared CB750 to eighth place in the 1970 Isle of Man 750cc Production TT. (Nick Nicholls)

privateers and teams such as the Dholda equipe run by Belgian dealer D'Hollander.

Nakamura had two Daytona Racers shipped to Honda France for the 1970 Bol d'Or, but while fast, they could not last the distance and Britain's Triumph team won.

A determined and successful CB750 racing campaign was staged by the Paris-based car and motorcycle dealer Japauto, thanks to the enthusiasm and wealth of its proprietor Christian Vilaseca. A remarkable character, whose other hobby was elephant hunting, Vilaseca was determined to achieve success, especially in the Bol d'Or.

Endurance racing rules were evolving away from the traditional production machine tradition and a Prototype class not requiring homologation of base production machines unleashed radical development and innovation.

Japauto began using enlarged 950cc engines from 1970 and soon moved into non-standard

territory with chassis built in the UK by London-based Dresda Autos. The result was a Bol d'Or win in 1972 against six other marques by Japauto riders Gerard Debrock and Roger Ruiz using a French-prepared CB750 engine with special internals.

Second and third places were also filled by Hondas, with Franco-Swiss pairing Georges Godier and Alain Genoud in second place on an Egli-framed machine followed by the British team of John Williams and Stan Woods on a machine prepared by Honda UK.

Debrock and Thierry Tchernine won a wet and windy second 'Bol' for Japauto in 1973, by which time the team had moved on to a French PEM chassis and adopted huge, distinctive fairings both for aerodynamic efficiency and to enhance rider comfort – highly important for performance in 24-hour racing. In 1975, the Japauto pairing of Ruiz and Christian Huguet triumphed in the FIM Coupe d'Endurance Championship. During the

following seasons, Japauto benefited from the arrival of a full works Honda endurance team, having access to RCB750 works engines. Interestingly, in 1976, Japauto raced with a heavily braced swingarm assembly which only needed one spring and damper unit.

Endurance racing had also caught on thousands of miles away in Australia. Named after its oil brand sponsor, the Castrol 1000 was inaugurated at Amaroo Park, Sydney in 1970, to be renamed the Castrol Six Hour after 1972. In the first event, a Honda CB750 ridden by New Zealander Craig Brown finished second overall behind a Triumph. In the televised 1971 race, however, the Honda-mounted team of Bryan Hindle and Clive Knight was victorious in the top capacity class, ahead of a 650cc Yamaha twin, with another CB750 in third spot.

Honda enters, Honda wins

In the early 1970s, official Honda machinery had only sporadic success in European endurance events and by 1975, the Kawasaki Z1 engine was becoming dominant. Keen to succeed in a sphere of international racing where four-strokes were still on top, Honda responded with a 749cc (66 x 54.76mm) works machine with three valves per cylinder known as the CB500 R, but it lacked torque and the solid reliability essential for success. Two of the 12-valvers started in the 1975 Bol d'Or, but retired.

Determined to put its stamp on the scene, in Autumn 1975 the factory launched a full factory team of double overhead camshaft racers derived from the CB750 and designed to run for stints of 5,000km (3,100 miles) without overhaul. Based in France, the equipe was called HERT (Honda European Racing Team) and was supervised by Michihiko Aika, boss of the Honda GP team before its disbandment eight years earlier. Management at events was by Honda France service chief, Jean-Louis Guillou.

The power unit of the devastatingly successful RCB was based on the CB750's bottom-end, but with massive straight-cut gears replacing the primary drive chains. These were responsible for a distinctive whine that warned other riders when they were about to be overtaken! In the upper engine twin camshafts

driven by a central duplex chain and spur gears operated four valves in each head. A self-generating ignition unit was sited behind the inclined cylinders and constant vacuum carburettors were chosen for flexibility and easy kick-starting in the absence of a heavy starter motor. Various sizes were used depending on the circuit, and they had lightweight bodies with transparent plastic floatbowls.

Despite the special specification, Honda was keen to suggest a strong link with the roadster. Factory machines were raced with engines of 915cc up to 1,024cc, but the machine's official designation was RCB750.

In 1976, engines of up to 954cc were raced in a purpose-built duplex tubular frame running on prototype Comstar wheels with Lockheed racing disc brakes front and rear. For 24-hour events, a lighting system powered two 55-watt Cibie front lamps in the fairing.

Endurance champion Jean-Claude Chemarin racing a 940cc RCB750 Four at the Thruxton round of the 1976 FIM Coupe d'Endurance where he teamed with US rider Pat Evans. They finished second behind the RCB of Christian Huguet and Roger Ruiz. (Nick Nicholls)

In its first season the mighty RCB swept to wins in all five FIM Coupe D'Endurance rounds. Riders included Honda France men Jean-Claude Chemarin, Christian Leon – winners of the FIM Championship from 1976 to 1979 – ex-Japauto men Christian Huguet and Roger Ruiz, as well as Britons Alex George, Charlie Williams and Stan Woods.

Adopting the slogan Honda Enters, Honda Wins, HERT swept to victory in 21 out of 24 events over four seasons. From 1977, uprated 997cc RCB750s were added to the team. They had a lower, more compact, frame with eccentric chain adjusters at the swingarm pivots and no less than 20kg (44lb) of weight was shed by various means, including replacement of the steel wheel spokes with alloy items, use of magnesium wheel hubs, carbon fibre in the fairing and seat mouldings and titanium for small components. For faster pit work, quick-release wheels were used, the rear one being removable without disturbing the drive chain.

More revisions followed for 1978 when the biggest-ever RCB750s with 1,084cc engines took the first three places in that year's Bol d'Or. Also in that race was an experimental high-revving RCB giving 140bhp. Ridden by US riders Dave Emde and Dale Singleton, it was there to counter the serious threat from a Yamaha TZ750 two-stroke specially prepared by the French Sonauto team. The aim was to set a really fast pace in the early stages in the hope of pushing the two-stroke to destruction, even if the RCB itself broke down. In the event, the US endurance novices finished in ninth place, the Yamaha blowing after 17 hours.

HERT was dissolved in 1979, but the CB900F-based 999cc RS1000 won the first full endurance world series in 1980. In the mid-1980s, Honda switched to V-four engine power for its big four-stroke racers, culminating in the World Superbike series-winning RVF750 RC45 of the 1990s.

Now preserved in Honda's museum, this 1977-type RCB750/1000 was raced by Honda Britain riders Charlie Williams and Stan Woods. (Honda)

Dirt demon

The CB750 engine was even tried in the peculiarly American sport of flat-track racing on dirt ovals. In 1974, Californian rider Rick Hocking rode a machine with a Yoshimura-tuned engine built into a dirt racing chassis by Doug Schwerma of Champion Frames, Hocking's co-sponsor with Rocky Cycle Accessories.

Although it was ridden hard in top-line national championship events on half-mile and one-mile tracks, the Champion Honda proved too heavy and wide to be really competitive. Also, while it was not short of speed, the Four's power characteristics were not as well suited to flat-track racing as that of its V-twin and parallel-twin rivals. Beast-tamer Rick Hocking went on to be the first of several riders to try Yamaha's TZ750 road-race engine on flat tracks in 1975, but after that season the AMA ruling body banned machines with more than two cylinders from dirt track events.

Several years later, Honda fielded official purpose-built RS750 V-twin engines to win four consecutive national dirt track championships from 1984 to 1987.

Rick Hocking slides his CB750-powered machine through a turn on the San Jose Mile flat track in 1974. (Dan Mahony)

Down the front straight, Hocking points down at the left side of his machine, indicating a problem. (Dan Mahony)

Successful formula

Gerald Davison of Honda UK was keen to raise the company's road racing profile in the mid-1970s. He felt the need to counter other players in the superbike market, but could not at first get a budget approved: 'In desperation, I talked to Dave Degens and as a result we built a racer from a CB750 used by our training school.'

The machine had a Dresda chassis similar to that provided by Degens for Japauto a few seasons before, while engine tuning included boosting the capacity to 900cc. Its livery was based on the Honda Style colours, with green and yellow stripes over the white base colour.

Former Ducati, Kawasaki and Triumph works rider Paul Smart (who had tested factory CB750 Racers with Sumiya in the USA in 1972, but had decided against racing the Honda Four) had a test ride, but felt that the Dresda Honda was not competitive enough for him.

In the event, two of the Honda Style racers were contested mostly by Degens himself and gained places in British short circuit events, mainly against Norton and Suzuki opposition.

Davison obtained a racing budget for 1977 and the Chiswick-based Honda Britain team was inaugurated. It was run by him, assisted by Alf Briggs and former John Player Norton teamster Norman White, who joined as chief mechanic, test rider and reserve team rider.

Its original rider team was Charlie Williams and Stan Woods, who had won the 1976 Barcelona 24 Hours marathon on a loaned Honda France machine, plus Geoff Barry, Roger Marshall and Tony Rutter.

The team, which was first supplied with an ex-Honda France 1976 RCB750 and later in the season a 1977 edition, only narrowly missed winning the 1977 Coupe d'Endurance series.

Special machinery was also prepared for a successful assault on the TT. The Isle of Man races lost their FIM world championship status after 1976, but as a concession to the circuit's unique status, TT Formula world titles were

The Egli-framed CB750 endurance racer campaigned by Frenchman Georges Godier and Swiss Alain Genoud, European endurance champions in 1972. Godier holds the machine in this photo taken in 1973 at Barcelona where the pair finished third. Swiss engineer Fritz Egli became a leading chassis maker after creating his own Vincent-powered racer in the 1960s and came to framing the CB750 engine via the CB450 twin. Egli's frames were characterised by a large-diameter oil-bearing main top tube running under the fuel tank. The Godier-Genoud team adopted Kawasaki power in 1974 and dominated the European endurance series for two seasons until Honda launched its factory campaign for 1976. Egli Motorteknik still flourishes today at Bettwill in Switzerland. (Mick Woollett)

René Guili on an official Honda France CB750 tended by
Japanese technicians at the 1970 Le Mans 1,000km race. It
finished in a lowly 12th place. (Alain Rouge)

Dave Degens on one of the Dresda-framed 900cc Honda Style
racers campaigned on UK short circuits. (Brian Holder)

instituted and originally run as one-round championships at the 1977 Isle of Man meeting. Despite its waning popularity with GP stars, the TT continued to be a showcase for manufacturers.

Davison had helped hatch the TT Formula concept, as it provided an opening for large-capacity four-stroke engines in two-stroke-dominated British racing.

To contest the TT Formula 1 race and championship, Honda Britain built a machine conforming to the rules allowing production roadster-based bikes of up to 1,000cc. Ridden to victory by seven-times GP World Champion Phil Read, it consisted of a 1976 RCB chassis fitted with a sohc CB750 F2-based engine. Bores were enlarged to 64mm to give 810cc and it was fitted

with one of the race kits supplied to the UK by Honda RSC. Riders not in the Honda team could only get access to kits through certain nominated dealers.

With the main team in Europe for an endurance round, the Formula 1 TT venture was in the hands of Honda UK employee Ken Hull, who worked for the race team outside of his 'day job' in the technical department.

Thirty-eight year old Read's TT comeback after five years' absence was controversial, since he had been vocal in criticising the circuit's safety, but had returned in response to financial incentives.

Read's win was also contentious in itself. Because of wet and deteriorating weather, the organisers decided to reduce the length of the

No fools

Power with flexibility made the CB750 engine a popular choice among sidecar road racers. In the mid-1970s, a trio of red and blue Honda-powered outfits was prominent in club events on the Southern UK circuits.

The three drivers calling themselves YAHTOF (Yet Another Hopeful Team of Fools) were Honda UK employee Ken Hull, Mick Barton and Reg Davies.

In the early 1970s, Hull had replaced Triumph twin power in his Fiddaman Kitten chassis with a Honda S800 car engine and a BSA gearbox. He made the outfit – called the *Shoestring 4* – competitive, winning club championships in 1974. But to keep pace with the opposition, especially the CB750 outfit of David Bexley, Hull switched to that unit. Hull recalled: 'I thought working for Honda would help in getting the parts I needed, but I ended up having to go through other suppliers.'

He joined forces with the other drivers in 1975 and despite its self-deprecatory name, YAHTOF set out to raise standards of professionalism in three-wheeled

Ken Hull and passenger Gerry Raymond-Barker aboard Hull's Honda-powered Fiddaman outfit. (Ken Hull)

race after it had started, the first time this had happened in a TT since 1954. Davison, who had flown in for the race heard from an official that the original five laps had been cut to four. He immediately made sure that Read was waved past the pits at the end of lap three, instead of being brought in to refuel as planned. With enough petrol on board to complete a fourth circuit, Read splashed on to take the win from Ducati-mounted Roger Nicholls.

The result drew an angry reaction from Nicholls' entrant, Steve Wynne of Sports Motor Cycles. His rider had been leading at the end of the third lap but made a fuel stop, since at that point, Wynne was unaware of the decision to shorten the race. Davison recalled: 'We were accused of cheating. But all I had done was bothered to leave the pits and ask the organisers what was happening.'

Hull remembered that the Honda had an empty oil tank when it took the chequered flag, thanks to a scavenging fault, and would not racing. Costs were shared and some backing provided by south-east London dealer Parks of Lewisham.

The outfits were all in red and blue, matching the team's transporter, an ageing Bedford Duple coach, while the crews wore uniform leathers.

The machines were all similar, having Fiddaman chassis powered by CB750 engines enlarged to 900cc with Keihin CR carburettors, Yoshimura camshafts driven by RSC kit chains, gas flowed heads, Lumenition optically triggered electronic ignition and close-ratio gearbox internals by Quaife.

Rarely out of the top three placings in club events, the team went well in 1975 until both Hull and Davies were sidelined by crashes. After recovering, Ken built a Gold Wing-powered outfit for 1976, but could not overcome crankshaft weaknesses and eventually fitted a 1,000cc CB750 unit.

Asked to join the Honda Britain race team in 1977, Hull decided to channel his love of speed into preparation rather than riding. He moved to the Mocheck team for 1978 and was involved in endurance racing into the 1980s. He now lives in Australia.

The YAHTOF Honda team line-up: three matching 900cc outfits and a transporter converted from a Bedford coach. (Ken Hull)

have run for much longer. Third was Ian Richards, who worked miracles on a 810cc Honda converted from road trim and entered by Midlands dealer Devimead. Fourth place went to Honda Britain teamster Stan Woods on an RSC-kitted 840 entered by Parks of Lewisham, but tended by Alf Briggs. Woods remembered: 'I lost time being slow to restart after my fuel stop. The other thing I recall was being right out of the seat when I had a "moment" at the fast School House corner left-hander going into Ramsey.'

Later in 1977, 21-year-old rising star Ron Haslam won the Formula 1 race run at the Silverstone John Player British GP on the ex-Read 820, and Woods was victor in a similar event at Brands Hatch.

In 1978, the TT was enlivened by the return of racing legend Mike Hailwood after 12 years' absence. There had been speculation that 'Mike the Bike' would ride for Honda, since he had won seven TTs for the factory in the 1960s. But well in advance of the event, Davison stated that

Read banks through the tight Ballacraine right-hander during the 1978 Formula 1 TT. He challenged Ducati-mounted Mike Hailwood for the lead before retiring with a bad oil leak. (Nick Nicholls)

he preferred to bank on Read for a second Formula 1 victory.

Faced by stiffening competition from rival UK-based Formula 1 teams, Honda Britain came to the line with a bigger, 969cc engine, said to give 95bhp and Read was backed up by two-times TT winner John Williams on a dealer-entered Honda. Hailwood accepted an offer to ride Sports Motorcycles' latest 862cc Ducati, prepared with limited factory assistance.

In a dramatic race Hailwood overtook Read, but the Honda rider pursued him doggedly and snatched the lead after their fuel stops. An estimated 40,000 spectators were treated to the sight and sound of the Ducati and the Honda racing in close company, but the dice ended when Read's machine began to smoke, slowed and then stopped on lap five. He explained: 'One of the oil cooler unions split. I was covered in oil and really fed up because I believed I had a chance of beating the Ducati, even though it had the edge on top speed, handled well and, of course, had Mike on board. But his engine broke crossing the finish line so if I had been able to keep the pressure on, it may have blown earlier.'

Honda gained some consolation from Williams's second placing, although he was two minutes behind the winner after being slowed by a loose fuel tank.

A Honda ridden by German TT ace Helmut Dahne took fourth spot behind Ian Richards' P&M Kawasaki. Built by German dealer Roland Eckert, Dahne's Four was one of a pair entered in the race. It had an 860cc engine and a special chassis giving extra suspension travel to suit the Isle of Man course. A Devimead CB750 raced by TT legend-to-be Joey Dunlop only completed four of the six laps.

Bob Hansen

An outstanding figure in American motorcycle racing history, Bob Hansen started out as a competitor on dirt tracks and in hill-climbs in the 1930s. He rode in his first Daytona 200 on a Norton in 1948, when the race was held on a mixed road and beach course.

He became a regular entrant during the 1950s and was admired for immaculately turned-out Indian, BSA and Matchless machines. In 1960, he was at Daytona with his BSA when he mentioned to his friend George French that he was going to open a motorcycle shop.

'George said why not handle Honda and I said: "What the hell is a Honda?" I put some in my showroom and they didn't leak oil on the floor. They sold quickly and we didn't see them again, because they didn't give any trouble.'

Convinced Honda had a great future, Hansen offered to be a parts distributor and as a result he was installed in a warehouse in Racine, Wisconsin to supply parts to the whole country east of the Mississippi river.

He continued being a race competitor and was in charge of Honda's entry of CB450 racers at Daytona in 1967, where one machine finished 10th in the 200-mile event.

By the time of the 1970 Daytona venture Hansen was based at American Honda's HQ in Gardena, California and was able to sit in on directors' meetings which were conducted in English for his benefit. Always ready to speak plainly and never a 'yes-man' Hansen had the ear of Mr Honda himself – allowing him to advocate the introduction of a four-cylinder model, during his factory visit early in 1968.

Bob believes the sudden ending of his employment at Honda following the CB750's Daytona victory was probably to do with him having given orders to Mr Nakamura in the dramatic closing stages of the race.

A lucrative Kawasaki contract beckoned and the Team Hansen 'Green Meanie' two-strokes became front runners in Formula 750 racing in the 1970s.

Honda invited Hansen to its 50th anniversary celebrations in 1998 however, showing the high regard in which he is still held for his contributions to the company's development.

Still absorbed in the challenges of track competition, Bob has been closely involved with the Heritage Racing project in recent years.

Bob Hansen during Heritage Racing's visit to the UK in 2001.
(John Colley)

In the early stages the race had been led by Irishman Tom Herron on a 941cc Honda entered by London Five Star Honda dealer Mocheck. But the Irish rider was sidelined when pounding from the Manx roads broke a rear shock absorber top mounting on the third of the six laps. A second Mocheck Honda finished eighth, ridden by Dennis Casement.

'That was the biggest disappointment ever for me: we should have won that race,' recalled Ken Hull, who after opting not to join the Honda Britain team as a full-time job for 1978, had taken charge of Mocheck's hardware. Financed by Mocheck's owners Ian Tay and Tony Ackner, the team fielded a pair of Fours finished in silver, yellow and orange. Assisted by Steve Baynam, Hull built them with British-made Omega pistons and Quaife close-ratio gearbox clusters, plus

Tom Herron accelerates his 810cc Mocheck Honda out of Quarter Bridge in the 1978 Formula 1 race. He looked set for a possible win or high placing, but retired with a broken frame. (Nick Nicholls)

Yoshimura cams. The chassis was provided by P&M, whose joint proprietor Richard Peckett had raced his own CB750-powered machine in previous seasons.

'The Mocheck bikes were very quick and steered really well,' recalled Hull, now resident in Australia. In fact, the dealer team beat Honda Britain in mainland events, leading to some discomfort for Hull in his office and a ban on assistance from official technicians. Mocheck's Tony Rutter had looked a likely British Formula 1 champion before being sidelined by a TT crash on another machine. His incapacity had led to Herron taking over his Formula 1 TT ride.

At the Ulster GP in August, Herron made amends for the TT retirement by winning the Formula 1 race ahead of Mocheck team-mate Rutter and John Williams, who had taken over the Honda UK machine after Read failed to complete

The two racers acquired from the factory by Bill Smith in 1972 being unloaded in Douglas harbour. When several of the Isle of Man Steam Packet ships did not have vehicle ramps it was usual to crane motorcycles on and off. (Steve Murray)

Mitch Boehm racing the Heritage Racing CB750 at Silverstone in 2001. (John Colley)

sufficient practice to be able to start in the event at the Dundrod circuit. It was the popular Williams's final meeting: he died following a crash on a Yamaha in the 1,000cc race held later.

After 1978, the homologation of Honda's dohc roadster fours made the CB750 obsolete in top-class racing, but several privateers soldiered on with it.

Still racing after all these years

When Dick Mann won the Daytona 200 for Honda in 1970, no-one could have foreseen that the CB750 would be winning races at the Florida circuit 30 years later. This extraordinary situation was made possible by the strength of America's vintage racing movement and the American Historic Racing Motorcycle Association (AHRMA) in particular.

Founded in the late 1980s to cater for growing numbers of riders wishing to compete in various branches of sport on obsolete machines, AHRMA runs a full season of road race meetings including a two-day extravaganza at Daytona during the annual springtime Bike Week. Honda

CB750s race in AHRMA's Formula 750 class for early 1970s four-strokes or accurate replicas of them. They also compete in multi-class Formula Vintage events.

American Honda played a part in the CB750's track revival when it set up Heritage Racing in 1996 on the run-up to the company's 1998 50th anniversary. One of the enthusiastic HR team's projects was a 750cc four built to contest AHRMA events and although official funding ceased, the team still campaigns it today.

Tended by Patrick Bodden of Washington DC, with assistance from Bob Hansen, the bike nicknamed 'Big Benly' is raced mainly by past Daytona winner Mitch Boehm, editor of *Motorcyclist* magazine. Although heavily modified, the Four contains few non-Honda parts, but has Lockheed twin-disc front brakes and a UK-made Nova close-ratio gearbox. The transmission is beefed up with Gold Wing clutch parts.

Said to give 92bhp at the rear wheel, Bodden's engine has a cylinder head tweaked by veteran tuner Curt Jordan and a CB750A crankshaft with Hy-Vo chain primary drive. Its exhaust system is copied from Sumiya's 1973 Daytona works

Heritage Honda boasts over 90bhp. (John Colley)

Alloy plates brace the swingarm to the engine. (John Colley)

machine and a Dyna ignition control box is positioned alongside the battery inside the seat tailpiece.

To improve handling, stout alloy plates brace the engine to the frame at the swingarm pivots and 3 metres of extra thin-walled tubing stiffens the frame, notably under the rearward part of the aluminium fuel tank. Other chassis parts are a pick'n'mix variety of Honda parts. For example, the rear wheel assembly combines a CB750 hub, CB550 disc, CB400F caliper, CB450 cush drive and VFR1000 brake torque arm, while the front fork combines components sourced from a Gold Wing and a CBX1000.

Former Heritage Racing teamster Mark McGrew split off in 1999 to form the rival M3 Racing team. Based in Minnesota, former American Honda employee McGrew started building himself a complete CB750 Racer with genuine parts in the late 1980s. The Barber Museum, America's most famous motorcycle collection, bought the finished article so McGrew began again and built the machine on which Adam Popp was to win several major AHRMA races.

Quoted as giving 'near' 100bhp at the rear wheel, the engine of Popp's mount has a McGrew-designed Web-Cam camshaft driven by a Tsubaki chain with flat-sided links running on a nylon slipper tensioner. A battery-powered Dyna electronic ignition also aids reliability, while carburation is by 31mm Keihin CR smoothbores as required by rules requiring the outward appearance to be as per the original.

Disc rear brake uses an amalgam of Honda parts.
(John Colley)

Internal engine tweaks include narrow-stemmed (5mm) valves, a lightened CB750A crankshaft, Wiseco pistons giving a 12.5:1 compression ratio and Nova gearbox internals. The open megaphone exhaust system was crafted in California by expatriate Briton Rob North, who made frames and other parts for BSA and Triumph's Daytona racers of 1970-71.

The frame has extra bracing around the swingarm pivots, to counter weave under acceleration that was particularly apparent at Daytona. Nitrogen rear suspension units, made for M3 by Works Performance, feature step-less pre-load adjustment and raise the rear end to add cornering clearance.

Twin front brake discs, skimmed to 5mm thickness and perforated, are mated with Grimeca two-piston calipers. The front fork has 37mm stanchions and CBX yokes which reduce trail. Rear braking at the rear wheel is by a replicated RSC-type twin-leading-shoe drum with a magnesium alloy backplate.

McGrew also races a Production class CB750 himself, and runs a second full-race machine first campaigned during 2001 by North Dakotan, John Staska.

Australia's lively historic racing scene has traditionally run a Post Classic category for machines dating from 1963 to 1972. In the Unlimited Post Classic races, Honda CB750s have been dominant and at times unbeatable.

Most successful have been potent tools campaigned by K&W Motorcycles of Melbourne and T-Rex racing. Their engines are enlarged to 970cc, 1,062cc and even 1,100cc, running on methanol, the alcohol-based fuel permitted in Australian historic racing.

Rider-engineer Rex Wolfenden, formerly of K&W and now proprietor of T-Rex, started road racing a Dresda-framed CB750 after a career in motocross. His 110bhp 970s, which have swept the board in several major Australian events, have CB1100 con-rods, locally made cams and valves, 31mm Keihin CRs and Dyna electronic ignition, setting its rev-limiter at

John Staska on the second M3 bike. Four-pipe systems are compulsory on CB750s in AHRMA competition. (John Colley)

World view

Vic World of San Carlos, California, is America's leading early CB750 specialist. His love of the Four dates back to the early Seventies, when his CB450 was off the road and he borrowed a friend's 750.

'From then on, I was addicted to the power,' recalled Vic who says he owns several sand-cast Fours, but is reticent about the exact number. One of them is the pre-production example featured on the cover of *Cycle Guide* in March 1969.

World Motorcycles has stockpiled a supply of 'new old stock' (NOS) spares. Vic began accumulating parts in the 1980s, searching inventory lists, acquiring dealers' stock and even buying as much as he could direct from Honda in Japan. His restorations even wear correct-period tyres.

After falling under the spell of the CB750 Racer legend, Vic set about converting a machine built in April 1969 to racing trim with genuine 970-series kit components.

'It took 10 years to collect 160 out of around 180 factory kit parts.'

His patience paid off in the spring of 2002 when the finished blue and silver machine won two AHRMA races at Daytona Speedway.

Another coup for the World equipe at the same event was the reuniting of Gary Fisher with the Krause Yoshimura Honda on which he had led the Daytona 200 race 30 years earlier. Restored and prepared for AHRMA racing by Vic, it was ridden to third place in the F750 and Formula vintage races by Fisher.

Back at Daytona in 2002, aboard the Yoshimura Honda restored by Vic World; Gary Fisher leads a Harley-Davidson rider. (World MCs)

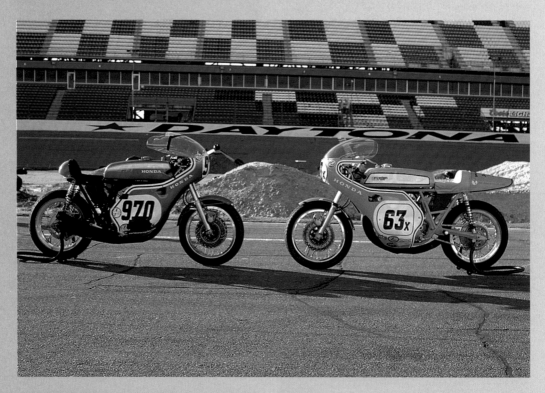

World's racers. The blue machine was built using genuine factory kit parts. (World MCs)

M3's number one uses many factory parts. (John Colley)

The replicated Honda twin-cam rear brake. (John Colley)

9,500rpm for safety. Strengthened frames are used with a box-section swingarm, Koni rear units, 18in wheels and Lockheed twin 300mm disc front brakes.

Other Honda Fours prepared by both Sharptune and K-Mach racing have also gained top results in Australian historic racing.

The CB750 has yet to make a real impact in historic racing on UK circuits. Several factors account for this. The Classic Racing Motorcycle Club has always discouraged four-cylinder machines and only admitted the Honda in 1997. Building a competitive CB750 is likely to be extremely expensive and the CRMC's historic Formula 750 class is dominated by fast riders on BSA and Triumphs which have been steadily improved over many seasons. The sure-handling triples are difficult to beat – as they were first time round. On short circuits without Daytona's full-bore expanses, the Honda's sheer power advantage is less usable.

The stock frame's steering angle is steepened. (John Colley)

M3's team. Mark McGrew is second from left, with John Staska and Adam Popp to his left. (John Colley)

At the time of writing, two CB750s were competing in CRMC events with a third being prepared. They were built in collaboration by club official Roger Bryant and seasoned racer Keith Soall. The latter reports seeing 78bhp in dynamometer tests from his 750cc machine which raced at Daytona in 2001. It has Keihin smoothbore carburettors, Yoshimura alloy con-rods, a Nova close-ratio gearbox, Bartel fuel tank and Maxton suspension. The third CB750 is the work of CRMC chairman Gordon Russell, who once built race engines for Honda UK.

Pete Rhodes, a Lancashire pioneer of Japanese bike restoration in the Eighties, more

One of the potent K&W racers in Australia. (Alan Cathcart)

CB750 Racer replica built by Pete Rhodes in 1996 for a collector. (Author)

recently replicated key racer kit parts and built up complete CB750 Racers using such parts.

Another British friend of the CB750 Racer is Bernie Saunders, a Gloucestershire garage owner who owns several historic Hondas, including a 1976 RCB and later 1,000cc and 1,123cc dohc fours. He restored Peter Darvill's 1970 CB750 which was second in the 1970 Bol d'Or, winning a major UK classic show concours award. Bernie has supplied parts and information to several other players in the CB750 racing world, including Heritage Racing and at the time of writing was restoring Darvill's two later works-framed endurance racers.

Not many people have been crazy enough to race the hefty CB750 in motocross, but AHRMA member Tom France from Haverstraw, New York, has attracted amazement and admiration in equal measure by campaigning one with a big-bore engine and box-section swingarm on the rough. His favoured technique is to make the quickest start off the line and take wide lines through turns, flinging up dirt and stones at following riders. (Matt Benson)

Converted roadsters in CRMC events. No. 54 is Keith Shoall's
and No. 6 belongs to club official Roger Bryant. (Author)

Riding CB750s today

The sheer numbers of Honda CB750s that were sold, along with the Four's outstanding ruggedness and reliability, has ensured the survival of many examples to the present day.

Ironically, the ascendancy of the 'Universal Japanese Motorcycle' following in the wake of the CB750 stimulated interest in preserving the less-sophisticated machinery of other makes made obsolete by the Honda.

A minority of motorcyclists, motivated by the notion that older machines possess special qualities such as 'character', which they find lacking in new products, constitutes a worldwide classic movement that has grown phenomenally since the late 1970s.

Twenty-five years on, the CB750 itself is rated as a desirable classic, a machine of distinction worthy of preservation. And rightly so, given the Four's tremendous importance in the history of the motorcycle and excellent performance for its age. Unlike some other products of its era, a properly looked after CB750 will reward its owner with many miles of brisk, pleasurable riding without the hassles of intensive maintenance and frequent breakdowns.

Easily capable of carrying one or two people and some luggage at the pace of modern traffic, the Four makes a supremely practical classic and benefits from better brakes and electrics than many other oldies.

It is not expensive to run, either. In some countries, a CB750's age will qualify it for road licence or tax concessions. In the UK, for example, a machine manufactured before January 1973 could, at the time of writing, be granted exemption from the substantial annual tax. Insurance costs can be drastically reduced if you take out a policy specifically for older machinery covering moderate annual mileages. Some policies are only available to members of particular clubs.

The cost of obtaining a machine varies greatly. Anyone determined to own a good specimen of one of the very earliest production CB750s with sand-cast engine cases will probably have to pay dearly for the privilege. To do justice to such a sought-after rarity, it would need to be maintained in excellent condition, but restoration to absolute originality is likely to be difficult because of the shortage of correct cosmetic parts. Later parts and their code numbers superseded earlier ones in Honda's spares inventory and the company eventually deletes items altogether. Components for CB750s are gradually being deleted and some parts for the pre-1971 models are definitely becoming scarce.

Although most of the K versions are less historic and exclusive, there are clear benefits of ownership. The purchase price is lower – really low if you are prepared to buy a rough example for restoration – and the machine incorporates

The author samples a 1970 CB750 superbly rebuilt to original condition in the UK by Rising Sun Restorations. Such a machine can offer many miles of enjoyment and will always attract admirers. (John Noble)

those refinements and reliability-enhancing modifications made by Honda during production. For the rider seeking the 'real' CB750 look combined with lively performance, the K1 and K2 are the best choice: many admirers of the Fours believe that the K2 is the best of all. Although the K1 was produced in the greatest numbers examples can be difficult to track down and, in the UK at least, K2s are easier to find.

The later Ks are now beginning to attract more buyers and while they don't have the same performance or charisma as the early examples, they offer high levels of comfort and refinement. Mid-series, K3 to K5 machines not originally marketed in Europe, are now widely spread across the globe thanks to the many traders who have, since the 1980s, been combing the United States for unwanted motorcycles and shipping them to Europe and Australia by the container-load.

Similarly, the K6 has practical virtues to be weighed up against its tendency to blandness,

while the final K7 and K8 don't have much of a following at all – yet, the latter model is very rarely seen in Europe.

Overshadowed in their day by more technically adventurous market rivals, the Super Sports have never been to the fore and are probably underrated as usable, enjoyable rides. The F and F1 are not only quick off the mark but stable at speed, although their busy power delivery and odd looks are not to everyone's taste. People seem particularly averse to the F1 Sulfur Yellow colour scheme.

The F2 and F3 offer more outright horsepower than the rest of the CB750s, although bottom-end pull is weak. Fuel economy is surprisingly good, as is roadholding, provided the FVQ rear units don't live up to their 'fade very quickly' nickname.

Riders could also regard their twin 275mm front discs as a practical plus as well, although the K-series and earlier Fs can be converted from a single to double-disc layout, a modification

Buyers beware! This CB750 at an Italian swap meet was claimed to be an early example, but its cylinder head was post-1973. (Author)

especially popular with France's numerous and enthusiastic K owners. Some riders find the braking from twin 300mm discs too ferocious.

The later Super Sport F2's and F3's looks, with their Comstar wheels, generally less-classic styling and black engine, will attract some buyers and repel others. So far, comparative disinterest in the F series has kept prices down.

Rarity, especially outside of America and Japan, gives the 750cc Hondamatics a certain exclusivity and any really dedicated CB750 collector will aspire to own one, or possibly all three variants, if only to complete their set. The drawbacks, apart from excessive bulk and a style of riding that may not suit the typical motor-cyclist, are expensive replacement parts and the complications of maintenance, repair and restoration.

Motorcycling journals and vehicle mart publications are the obvious place to look for secondhand machinery, but remember that real discoveries and bargains often turn up in the classified advertisements of local newspapers and even on supermarket notice boards. Members of clubs – CB750 owners are well catered for by several organisations worldwide – are well positioned to hear of good buys and simply letting it be known among friends and associates that you are looking for something specific can bear fruit sooner or later.

Shows, autojumbles and swap meets are another source of machines. It pays to go early in the day, and to take along a knowledgeable friend who is sceptical enough to hold you back from making a rash move. This is especially important if you are in a foreign country and are not fluent in the language. Similarly, auctions can throw up horrors as well as genuine treasures. It pays to study a machine thoroughly, demand to see documents and ask probing questions.

Nowadays, internet auction sites such as eBay are also a potentially rich source for motorcycles, parts and literature, although transactions are often made on trust.

All the normal things a secondhand motor-cycle buyer should be aware of apply to the CB750. Look for signs of poor maintenance or downright abuse, which might include chewed heads on screws and other fasteners, frayed cables, a slack drive chain and hooked sprocket teeth. The popularity of the Fours meant that a high proportion were owned by riders who did not have the feel for mechanical things which characterises many dedicated motorcyclists. Smart paintwork is no guarantee that engine oil is clean. Some consequences of neglect, such as engines seizing or brakes failing, can be extremely dangerous.

Deviations from standard handlebars, seats, mudguards, exhaust systems and carburettors are all likely to cause extra problems if you ultimately want a perfectly standard machine and calculations need to be made about the cost of

rectifying alterations. But don't forget that if a machine has been kitted with parts by Dresda, Dunstall, Rickman, Seeley, Yoshimura or another well-known aftermarket supplier, and is in generally good condition, it could be valued in its existing form as an authentic period piece.

Among the things to check out on the CB750 particularly are signs of welded-up crankcase damage in the area of the front drive sprocket, the legacy of a past chain breakage. Inspection will mean removing the small sprocket cover plate and possibly cleaning away residues of chain lubricant inside. If a satisfactory repair has been made, there should be no problem. Oil leaks will usually indicate that there is cause for concern: it is not unknown to find rough and insufficient owners' repairs carried out with body repair paste or silicon caulk. Be warned: chain breakages do still occur on early machines.

Readers' ratings

In June 1979, the CB750 was the subject of UK monthly *Motorcycle Mechanics*' series in which readers were asked to assess their own machines.

The respondents had an average age of 23 with just under seven years of riding experience and had owned their CB750 for just over a year. Half used their Hondas as their sole means of transport.

Almost half carried out their own maintenance, while 22 per cent left it entirely to dealers. The majority had bought their mounts new and mileages ranged from 500 to 42,000.

Most expressed satisfaction at the Four's speed and acceleration, happy that the Honda could cruise at 80mph (130km/h) without being stretched yet could accelerate as hard as required when necessary. However, some owners pointed out that using the performance available was heavy on fuel, tyres and chains. Typical mileage figures were 4,500–6,000 for a rear tyre, 14,000 for a front tyre and 6,000 for a pre-O-ring drive chain. Average fuel consumption was 45-50mpg (6-5.5 litre/100km).

Handling was generally rated highly, although some riders reported slight wobbles at low speed and others detected a high-speed weave. The tendency to fall into slow corners was widely reported as was awkwardness in slow traffic.

There was little agreement over suspension: some said it was too soft, while others thought it firm. Discomfort after covering over 150 miles was mentioned as was tingly vibration felt through the passenger footrests at mid and high rpm.

Reliability came out clearly as one of the model's most admired attributes, with respondents describing it as 'perfect' and 'excellent'. Ease of maintenance was rated lower, mainly because owners found tappet and timing adjustment tricky and that tools supplied with the machine were only suitable for the most basic maintenance. Most relied on dealers to carry out carburettor balancing.

Popular non-standard modifications included, fitting Cibié sealed-beam headlamps, Girling or Koni rear units, and Avon or Dunlop tyres.

All but one owner said they would recommend the CB750 to a friend and most said they would happily buy another, although in reality they intended moving on to a different model. Fifty per cent intended to stick with Honda.

Dents can sometimes be found on the frame front downtubes near the exhaust ports. These are the result of using a steel bar to brutally lever off an aftermarket four-into-one system, which can be difficult to shift because the stubs in the head are not parallel but slightly splayed relative to each other.

Freedom from oil leaks was one of the Honda's big advantages over British twins and triples, but early CB750s tended to develop a slight weep at the head joint. An extra holding-down bolt was introduced early in production and several changes were made to head gasket specifications. Leaking at the joint can also be caused by deterioration of the neoprene O-rings which seal oil passages at the joint and will be cured by replacement.

Naturally, engine and frame numbers should be checked against the records to see if they correlate. Machines sold in the US market should have a vehicle identification number (VIN) plate riveted to the right side of the steering head and information carried on it includes the date of manufacture. The factory-stamped frame number is on the left side of the steering head and the engine number should be easily seen on the left side main casing.

While many buyers prefer to know they have a machine that is complete as manufactured, there is no reason why a bike, which has had new main cases fitted after a chain breakage or a full engine change after a mechanical disaster should not perform reliably in otherwise good condition. Sometimes, a past engine switch is indicated by the post-1973 cylinder head finning pattern on an older machine.

The metal pan that forms the base of the seat is likely to be attacked by rust and the earliest seat fillings were a type of red foam which hardens and crumbles to dust as it ages. While the seat is lifted, check for corrosion damage on the chromed metal portion of the rear mudguard.

On a Comstar wheel, look for corrosion caused by electrolytic action where the steel and aluminium is riveted together. If you suspect a Comstar to be out-of-true, it need not be terminal, as in many cases the better specialist wheel repair companies can rectify such problems.

Taking a beaten-up machine to a professional restorer can be the easiest route to having a gleaming as-new machine that runs sweetly, but it can also be costly. Check that your chosen practitioner knows the model well and be sure of the likely costs before work starts.

Some of the nicest restored CB750s around are the work of owner-restorers, but considerable skill, knowledge and patience are required to achieve their high standards.

When buying genuine Honda spares, it pays to seek out a specialist supplier who is familiar with and sympathetic towards long-obsolete machinery.

Finding the necessary parts is becoming more difficult all the time and supplies of certain CB750 components are now being deleted by Honda. But all sorts of things are still turning up at jumbles and swap meets: a brand-new boxed cylinder head was found by a restorer and bought at very reasonable cost at the time this was written.

Typical corrosion has set in on the metal part of the rear mudguard under the seat on this 1970 model. (John Colley)

Clubs and individuals sometimes come to the rescue by arranging to have parts in short supply manufactured, typical examples being seat covers and early air boxes. On the whole, however, it is best to seek genuine Honda parts where possible and owning the parts book for the model you are working on will prove extremely useful. For models of the later 1970s, you may only be able to find parts lists in microfiche form but second-hand fiche readers

UK owner David Sketchley bought this US-market K5 and found he rode it more than his Ducati Monster S4. (John Colley)

Converting to twin-disc front brakes using standard calipers is a fairly common modification. (John Colley)

are often advertised in family history magazines.

The parts book clearly explains the Honda parts numbering system introduced from 1966, which is simple to comprehend and based on groups of digits. For model-specific parts the first group, usually five digits, is the individual component number and after that comes the factory model code. The third grouping is used to indicate an update and

where applicable an outside supplier's code, while letter suffixes following the numbers indicate a colour.

An example would be 83600-341-701LV, describing a left side panel for a CB750 K3 or K4 in Flake Sunrise Orange.

The most common model codes you will encounter are:

CB750-CB750 K1	300
CB750 K2 - K6	341
CB750 K7 -K8	405
CB750 F-F1	392
CB750A	393
CB750 F2-F3	410
CB750 Racer	300–970

Found languishing in a shop by CB750 collector Eamon Maloney, this F2 turned out to be an ex-Honda UK test machine. He reports sizzling performance and is restoring it to its original black colour scheme. (John Colley)

Combing through heaps of parts like this at swap meets and auto jumbles is all part of the fun for keen restorers. (Author)

Parts general to various models such as nuts, bolts and washers are listed under two group numbers. The first group is the part's own number while the second details dimensions and thread types.

As was mentioned earlier, many parts and their numbers were updated. If you order a genuine Honda seat for a CB750 K2, it will conform to the K6 pattern.

Some of the most immaculately finished CB750s around are built primarily for entry in shows and concours d'elegance competitions, where perfect finish and absolute originality are paramount. Their restorers take trouble over the minutest detail, even ensuring that the various warning stickers Honda was fond of applying are correct for the market a machine was originally supplied to. The CB750 was made in such large volumes that a lifetime could be spent identifying every last variation between individual machines.

Show bikes may be fitted with well-preserved examples of original fitment tyres, but any machine intended for road riding must wear tyres of more recent manufacture to be safe. Some tyre makers quote their products' maximum safe life as seven years.

There are different schools of thought about which tyres best suit CB750s. Most riders agree that handling is better, as it is on several large-capacity machines of the period, with a ribbed front cover. But some are satisfied with the ride given by the Dunlop K81 TT100 with identical front and rear tread patterns. Among the pairs available in the usual CB750 19-inch front and 18-inch rear sizes with ribbed front treads are good quality tyres from the German companies Continental and Metzeler.

Honda-mad Max

Max on the road with his beautifully restored K2. (John Colley)

One down, at least six to go. Max's first CB750 restoration indicates that the others will be beauties as well. (John Colley)

One of Britain's most enthusiastic CB750 riders and restorers is South Yorkshireman Max Elliot. A man with a keen interest in history, Max has also been involved in recovering and restoring a crashed Second World War Spitfire aircraft.

His concours competition-winning Candy Sunrise Orange K2 is an American market machine brought to Britain by import specialist A&P from whom Max bought it in 1999. Although its engine was partially seized and there were 50,000 miles recorded, the internals were found to be basically sound.

'I think it would have gone another 25,000 without a full rebuild. The CB750 was probably the first motorcycle to be capable of car-type mileages,' suggests Max, who opted instead to renew all the bearings and other critical parts in the power unit. He converted to an O-ring chain and it runs on Continental Super Twin tyres: 'They look the part, but they are also nice and sticky,' he says.

He was 16 years old and on trainee wages when the CB750 first appeared but obtained the model he'd always wanted after completing his first restoration of a Honda CB350 K4. Max now assiduously collects spares from a variety of sources, building up stocks to feed a conveyor belt of restoration projects.

At the time of writing Max had a K1, three K3s, a K4 and a K5, all at various stages of redemption. He is helped by sharing information with his Sheffield-based friend Chris Rushden, knowledgeable owner of many Hondas and several CB750s including a sand-cast type on which he's covered 30,000 miles.

Max's modern Honda is an imported Japanese-market CB1300 Super Four, which he loves, especially for its stupendous 88ft lb of torque.

'When I look at it, I can see a lot of similarities with the old Fours. Even the choke control is down on the left side where it is on my K1.'

Younger cousin: Max sees his CB1300 Super Four as a present-day equivalent of the original CB750. (Author)

Oil is a matter of personal choice, the original
recommended multigrades being SAE10W40
or SAE25-50. Regular oil and filter changes are
absolutely vital and worth the time, trouble and
cost in terms of looking after your engine. Use
only a reputable brand of oil filter and as well
as emptying the tank during changes, don't
forget to drain off the half litre or so of oil that
settles inside the crankcase. The official
change interval is 1,500 miles which can be
irksome for the high-mileage rider, but some
owners play ultra-safe and change at 1,000
miles; a good plan if the bike is only used for
short trips. During production, small metering
jets were introduced in the oilways which
supply the top end of the engine. If these are
clogged by dirt or sludge a seized camshaft
could be the result.

The engine must be removed to gain access
to the camshaft, but unlike many other Honda
engines, the CB750 does not run the camshaft
directly in the head casting, so seized bearings
are relatively simple to repair. For a bike that will
be used, it makes sense to fit an O-ring drive
chain conversion to the pre-1977 models to be
sure of long service.

The camshaft chain is self-tensioning. The drill
is to loosen the adjuster bar's locking bolt, turn

Each variant (except the model called K0 in the UK) has its
own owner's manual. The model code is on the back cover.
(John Colley)

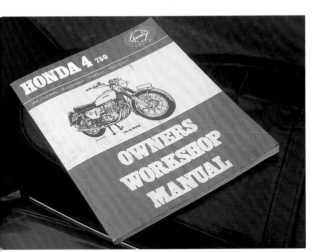

A Haynes Manual is invaluable; this 1974 edition is now a collector's item in its own right! (John Colley)

Title documents make life easier when applying for an age-related registration on an imported machine. (John Colley)

A good quality battery kept in good condition will ensure instant starting from cold. (John Colley)

the engine to a point where all its valves are closed and retighten the adjuster without applying any other pressure to the chain.

You are likely to find extra holes cut in air boxes, but such modification is not recommended. Only one of the carburettors is inhaling at any given time and the stock apertures are quite large enough. However, some specialists believe that on CB750 and K1

Fours supplied on the French, Dutch, German and European Direct markets, changing to the UK/US market type of box and element will give a noticeable performance improvement. Genuine Honda elements are intended to be cleaned by blowing through with an air line and re-used. Many owners endorse the well-proven American K&N brand of element, which is also meant to last indefinitely.

If a high-quality battery is fitted and kept in good condition using one of the excellent modern chargers specifically designed for motorcycles, starting should be totally reliable. However, if a machine stands unused for several months the carburettor float bowls should be drained and cleaned and stale petrol in the tank replaced by a fresh fill.

The constituents of fuel have changed considerably since the 1970s, but normal unleaded petrol is satisfactory for all the Fours in standard form.

All-weather riding can present problems, notably ignition troubles caused by rain water getting into the under-tank ignition switch or shorting out the plugs. The steel-encased spark plug caps used on earlier Fours are particularly vulnerable to shorting-out. Corrosion can seize

Londoner Eamon Maloney riding one of his two F2s. He also owns an F1 and several K models as well as a 1970 CB750.
(John Colley)

the front brake caliper bracket on its pivot pin. Some owners fit a grease nipple here to prevent this. Road salt can also cause trouble if it penetrates between the rear brake's iron liner and the alloy hub, so this assembly should be closely examined. On models with disc rear brakes, these should also be checked for the effects of winter corrosion. The F and F1 models were notorious for collecting rain water in the storage box under the seat tailpiece.

Certain minor faults are normal. As on many Hondas the gearchange can be notchy when riding at low speeds. On early machines with the UK-layout right handlebar switch it is possible to select the pilot light position between the main and dip positions which, turns off the headlamp: something to guard against when riding at night! A certain amount of mechanical noise from the engine is inevitable: our expectations in this

respect have been greatly raised in the years since 1969.

In rainy Britain, performance of the front brake was often impaired by water until it had been applied a few times or held on very lightly for a short period. However, modern brake pads with sintered friction linings are a great improvement over the period components in this, and other, respects.

If you don't mind using non-standard equipment, the rear suspension can be improved by fitting aftermarket units recommended for the model in question. This was common practice among discerning riders when the 750s were current. However, first check that handling quirks are not being caused by worn steering head bearings, which can be replaced by tapered-roller units, and check for wear at the swingarm pivot bushes. When a

One for the road

Tuning is mild, but Clive Brooker's special has authentic racer looks and brisk performance. (Pete's Pictures)

This mouth-watering road-legal CB750 Racer is the work of Clive Brooker, a 45-year-old motorcycle technician and former employee of Phil Read International from Kent. Based on a 1972 CB750 K2, it took 18 months to build. The engine cases were lightened, the standard crankshaft polished and the connecting rods X-rayed to check for cracks. A heavy-duty cam chain is fitted, cam timing altered, and heavy-duty springs used with polished valves. Standard carburettors were re-jetted to suit bellmouth intakes that replaced the air filter. To cut weight, the starter motor was removed and the battery was put in its place.

The fuel and oil tanks, seat, fairing and screen were supplied by Bartel Engineering. Both wheels have Italian aluminium rims and the front disc brake is doubled up using stock calipers. Pleased with his creation, Clive said: 'It looks good, goes really good and the four-into-one big-bore exhaust sounds great.'

Electrical components are tucked inside the seat hump. Lights and number plate are a concession to road rules.
(Pete's Pictures)

Modern descendants

The early 1990s saw the sudden rise in popularity of the Retro. So called because its styling harked back to an earlier period, it dispensed with many of the developments applied to mainstream Japanese motorcycles in the 1980s. Typically, the Retro lacks fairings, has an air-cooled engine, a tubular frame and twin-shock swingarm rear suspension. A useful all-round machine, it is relatively cheap to manufacture and can be sold at an attractive price.

The CB Seven-Fifty was launched in Japan in 1992 and elsewhere later. Honda evoked the original CB750 Four in extolling its virtues in sales literature.

The modern incarnation owes more in design terms to the post-1978 style of Honda in-line four, being powered by a 748cc over-square 67 x 53mm engine with twin overhead camshafts and four valves per cylinder. Easy use, town or country practicality, a minimum maintenance programme and comfort for one or two riders are qualities claimed for the original CB750. The current machine is even said to carry an echo of the old Four in its exhaust note, although much more stringent emissions regulations apply today. Power output of the Seven-Fifty is 73bhp at 8,500rpm giving a maximum speed of just over 120mph (190km/h).

At the Tokyo Show of 1999, Honda marked the 30th anniversary of the original CB750's debut by displaying a prototype called the CB Four, housing a twin-cam 750cc in-line four-cylinder engine in cycle parts that echoed the 1969 original. These included a chromed four-pipe exhaust system with megaphone silencers, a round headlamp, fork gaiters and plain, undrilled rotors for the twin-disc front brakes. The fuel tank striping and badges were also evocative of the old-style Four.

Practical rather than exciting, the CB Seven-Fifty has been in the Honda range since 1992. (Honda)

Retro-style CB Four with a dohc engine, displayed at the 1999 Tokyo Show. (WMCNA)

The early 300-series silencer, on left, has a detachable baffle with release bolt and larger outlet than the K2's 341-series type. (John Colley)

For detail fanatics: the alternator cover on the left has recesses for mounting screw heads, which were absent in the very early type. (John Colley)

A plated rear lamp and licence plate holder for the K2-on. UK models have a black-enamelled type. (John Colley)

A smaller K3/K4 indicator unit next to the bigger US-market K5 item, shared with the GL1000 Gold Wing. (John Colley)

Seat cover patterns were regularly altered, although the base was changed less. This unrestored seat is for the K3. (Author)

US-market headlight switches lacked the central park position seen on the UK version. This unit was adopted from the K5. (John Colley)

Introduced on the K5, this side stand has a rubber extension designed to flip it up safely if accidentally left extended. (John Colley)

From 1972 on, the K-series frame has a brake pedal stop welded to a gusset plate near the right-side swingarm pivot. (John Colley)

Sprockets: the 48-tooth type used from the K1 with the early 45-tooth wheel, which is getting harder to find now. (John Colley)

The speedometer type fitted to the K3 only, with a rubber anti-vibration cushion. The dial has a red line at 70mph. (John Colley)

The front brake lever assembly. The lettering on the master cylinder cap varied: this is correct for US-market K3s to K5s. (John Colley)

The tank for the K4 in Boss Maroon colour option. It has the two-handed fuel filler cap introduced for safety from 1972. (John Colley)

CB750: slotted side panel. (John Colley)

K2: black centered tank trim. (John Colley)

CB750: UK headlamp switch. (John Colley)

K2: VIN plate on US version. (John Colley)

K2: warning lights panel. (John Colley)

K5: black front brake caliper. (John Colley)

K5: large US market rear lamp. (John Colley)

K3: gold ground in Honda Wing badge. (John Colley)

K7: passenger footrest above the silencers. (John Colley)

K7: flush filler cover on the fuel tank. (John Colley)

F1: large silencer and footrest hanger plate. (John Colley)

F1: warning lights panel. (John Colley)

F2: tank badge and paint scheme. (John Colley)

F2: water gutter above the rear disc. (John Colley)

F2: front brake caliper and black fork slider. (John Colley)

CB750A: tank-top warning stickers. (John Colley)

machine is being rebuilt or fitted with an endless chain, these should be greased.

Proprietary exhaust systems, whether patterned on the original or converting to a four-into-one layout, will prove much less expensive than replacing with original parts, if indeed you can obtain them. The megaphone-style silencers used up to the K6 were prone to rotting, especially if machines were mainly used for short journeys, the upper left one often being the first to suffer.

A points-less electronic ignition system will not change the machine's outward appearance and dispenses with the need for contact breaker points adjustment. It also keeps the spark timing dead consistent on all four cylinders, contributing to sweet and smooth running.

Overall gearing can be changed using proprietary sprockets. It is worth noting that the CB750 rear sprocket can last many miles – over 30,000 in some cases – without serious wear.

Motorcyclists who are only familiar with four-cylinder machines of the last 10 years might not be too impressed by a ride on a Honda CB750, finding it relatively sluggish, rather top heavy, mechanically noisy and poorly braked. That goes to show how much technical progress has been made over 30 years. But there is no doubt that the Honda milestone of 1968 made a huge contribution to the achievement of such sophistication. If any youthful riders need proof of that, they should also try rapidly covering 100 miles on a typical 750cc parallel twin of the Sixties.

Appendix

Specifications
CB750

Engine:	air-cooled single overhead camshaft 8-valve in-line four			
Cubic capacity:	736cc			
Bore and stroke	61 x 63mm			
Compression ratio:	9:1	F-F1, K7-K8: 9.2:1	F2-F3: 9:1	A-A2: 8.6:1
Inlet valve size:	32mm	F2-F3: 34mm		
Exhaust valve size:	28mm	F2-F3: 31mm		
Camshaft drive:	single-row chain			
Carburation:	4 x 28mm 28 Keihin PW	K7-K8, F2-F3: 4 x 28mm Keihin PD, A-A2: 4 x 24mm Keihin PD		
Air filtration:	micronic element			
Lubrication system:	dry sump with filtration	A-A2: wet sump		
Oil capacity:	3.5 litres	A-A2: 5.5 litres		
Generator:	210W alternator			
Battery:	12-volt, 14-amp hour			
Ignition:	coils and twin contact breakers			
Maximum power:	67bhp @ 8,000rpm	F2-F3: 70bhp @ 9,000rpm	A-A2: 47bhp @ 7,500rpm	
Maximum torque:	6.12kg m @ 7,000rpm	F2-F3: 5.9kg m @ 7,500rpm	A2: 5kg m @ 6,000rpm	
Primary drive:	2 x single-row chains	A-A2: Hy-Vo chain		
Clutch:	wet, multiplate	A-A2: 2 x hydraulic		
Gearbox:	five-speed constant-mesh	A-A2: two-speed semi-automatic		
Final drive:	chain	K7, F1-F3, A-A2: self-lubricated chain		
Frame:	tubular steel, double cradle			
Front suspension:	telescopic fork, 35mm tube			
Rear suspension:	swingarm, twin shocks			
Front wheel:	19in spoked, steel rim	F2-F3: 19in composite	A-A2: 19in spoked, alloy rim	
Rear wheel:	18in spoked, steel rim	F2-F3: 18in composite	K7, A-A2: 17in spoked, alloy rim	
Front brake:	296mm disc	F2-F3: 2 x 275mm discs		
Rear brake:	180mm drum	K7 (Japan), F1-F3: 300mm disc		
Front tyre:	3.25 x 19in	K7: 3.50 x 19in		
Rear tyre:	4.00 x 18in	K7, A-A2: 4.50 x 17		
Wheelbase:	1,455mm	K7-K8: 1495mm	F-F1: 1475mm F2-F3: 1,480mm	A-A2: 1480mm
Seat height:	800mm	K7: 810mm	F2-F3: 830mm	A-A2: 838mm
Ground clearance:	160mm	K6: 140mm,	K7-K8: 150mm F-F3: 135mm	A-A2: 190mm
Overall width:	885mm	K6: 870mm	K7-K8: 880mm F-F3: 860mm	A-A2: 880
Dry weight:	218kg	K7-K8: 231kg	F-F1: 244kg F2-F3: 250kg	A-A2: 262kg
Fuel capacity:	16 litres	F1-F3: 18 litres	K7: 17 litres	A-A2: 19 litres
Top speed:	124mph (200km/h)	K1-K7: 110mph (185km/h) F1: 115mph (185km/h)		
		F2-F3: 120mph (193km/h) A-A2: 100mph (156km/h)		

CB750 Racer, factory type

Capacity:	748.6cc*
Bore x stroke:	61.5 x 63mm*
Compression ratio:	10.5:1–11:1
Carburation:	4 x 31-35mm Keihin CR
Ignition:	magneto
Maximum power:	92bhp @ 9,500rpm (1973: 100PS @ 9,000rpm)
Gearbox:	five-speed, close ratio
Clutch:	wet, multi-plate
Front brake:	2 x 296mm discs
Rear brake:	200mm twin-leading-shoe drum
Dry weight:	155kg
Top speed:	164mph/264km/h (estimated)

* Daytona rules allowed cylinders to be bored to their maximum service oversize

1976 RCB750 Endurance racer, code 480/481

Engine:	air-cooled double overhead camshaft 16-valve in-line four
Capacity:	915cc/941cc
Bore x stroke:	68 x 63mm/68 x 64.8mm
Compression ratio:	11:1
Camshaft drive:	duplex chain and straight-cut gears
Lubrication system:	dry sump with cooling radiator
Carburation:	4 x 31/33/35mm Keihin CV
Ignition:	magneto
Maximum power:	111bhp @ 9,500rpm/116bhp @ 9,000rpm
Primary drive:	straight-cut gears
Gearbox:	five-speed, close ratio
Clutch:	wet, multi-plate
Fuel capacity:	24 litres
Oil capacity:	7 litres
Front brake:	2 x 296mm discs
Rear brake:	296mm disc
Dry weight:	190kg/195kg
Top speed:	170mph/274km/h (estimated)

1977–78 RCB1000 Endurance racer, code 481A/482

Capacity:	997cc
Bore x stroke:	70 x 64.8mm
Compression ratio:	10.5:1
Carburation:	4 x 35mm Keihin CV
Ignition:	CDI electronic
Maximum power:	120bhp @ 9,000rpm/135bhp @ 10,000rpm
Maximum torque:	10kg m @ 8,000rpm/11kg m @ 8,500rpm
Dry weight:	175kg/182kg
Top speed:	175mph/282km/h (estimated)

Road models 1969 to 1978

Guide to serial numbers, dates and approximate production figures

CB750 (1969–1970)
Frame: from 1000001
Engine: from E 1000001
Total: 53,400

CB750 K1 (August 1970–November 1971)
Frame: from 1044650
Engine: from E 1044806
Total: 77,000

CB750 K2 (November 1971–September 1972)
Frame: from 2000001
Engine: from E 2000001
Total: 63,500

CB750 K3 (September 1972–June 1973)
Frame: from 2200001
Engine: from E 2200001
Total: 38,000

CB750 K4 (June 1973–May 1974)
Frame: from 2300001
Engine: from E 2300001
Total: 60,000

CB750 K5 (May–December 1974)
Frame: from 2500001
Engine: from E 2372115
Total: 35,000

CB750 K6 (December 1974–June 1976)
Frame: from 2540001
Engine: from E 2428762
Total: 42,000

CB750 K7 (June 1976–May 1977)
Frame: from 2700002
Engine: from E 2700001
Total: 38,000

CB750 K8 (May 1977–May 1978)
Frame: from 2800001
Engine: from E 3000001
Total: 36,000

CB750 F (January–February 1975)
Frame: from 100.00.02
Engine: from 250.00.04
Total: 15,000

CB750 F1 (March 1975–November 1976)
Frame: from 200.00.03
Engine: from 251.50.94
Total: 44,000

CB750 F2 (November 1976–May 1977)
Frame: from 210.00.11
Engine: from 260.00.04
Total: 25,000

CB750 F3 (May 1977–May 1978)
Frame: from 220.00.01
Engine: from 310.00.01
Total: 18,400

CB750A (December 1975–September 1976)
Frame: from 7000001
Engine: from E 7000001
Total: 4,100

CB750 A1 (September 1976–May 1977)
Frame: from 7100001
Engine: from E 7100001
Total: 2,300

CB750A2 (May–October 1977)
Frame: from 7200001
Engine: from E 7200001
Total: 1,700

Index